Reclaiming Our Voices

An anthology honoring survivors of domestic violence and sexual assault

"Trigger Warning": This content deals with accounts of sexual assault
and domestic abuse and may be triggering to some people.

Editing by Carla Christopher-Waid,
 T.L. Christopher-Waid, Kate Harmon and Michelle
Cooper
Graphic Design, Layout and Cover by Carla
Christopher-Waid and T.L. Christopher-Waid
Printed in the United States for Community Arts Ink
York, PA   www.communityartsink.org

ISBN-13: 978-0692405741
ISBN-10: 0692405747

Contents

Introduction

As advocates for survivors of domestic and sexual violence, we see firsthand how abuse creates silence. We see countless women become mute with fear when asked to talk about what happened to them. We see mothers and fathers at a loss for words when facing the reality of their child's death at the hand of a domestic partner. Most often, we see bystanders unable to offer support to those who suffer at the hands of their abuser, or the memories that continue to haunt them, because abuse has stolen their voices too.

Domestic violence and sexual assault are portrayed very dramatically on TV, and newspaper articles tend to focus on only the most brutal cases; when the abuse we are faced with doesn't match those interpretations, we, as a society, have a tendency to dismiss it. Abuse is not always physical. Sexual assault is not always rape. 90% of people who are transgender or gender non-conforming report being sexually harassed at some point in their lives; this includes verbal harassment, threats, discrimination, and physical assault. 1 in 4 women will experience some form of abuse in their adult life; many who report being emotionally abused, including threats against their lives or the lives of their children, are unable to receive protection because their concerns are not taken seriously.

It is because of this that we here at ACCESS- York and the Victim Assistance Center celebrate this anthology. We celebrate these brave, strong souls who have found a way to stand up to violence by finding the voice that it so desperately tried to silence. We want everyone to read this book, because it truly is for all of us; survivors, their loved ones, community members...everyone. We all have the opportunity to find our voice, be it by telling our story, supporting someone else's effort to do so, or by raising our voices together against abuse of any kind.

Richard Azzaro
ACCESS York
YWCA York

ACCESS-York &
Victim Assistance Center
eliminating racism
empowering women **ywca**

A LETTER NO FATHER WANTS TO WRITE

(A fictitious letter based upon real experiences)

To My Daughter,
Let me begin by saying that I am so proud of you. You have met the challenges in your life with colossal strength and conviction. At times I forget you are not a little girl anymore. You grew up so fast. It seems like only yesterday that I took off your training wheels as you ventured out with two wheels to explore the world.
Before I knew it, you were a young lady with your own thoughts and dreams.

I am not sure you can fully understand how a man changes when blessed with a daughter. With a new perspective and a softening of the heart, dads often stumble through.

I honestly did not know what to think, feel or do when you so bravely told us about your unspeakable rape. I still find it extremely difficult to understand and accept. No father wants his daughter to be a victim of rape. A father is told that he is supposed to protect his daughter from the many threats he knows all too well.
I still ask myself, "Could I have done anything to prevent this from happening?" I was not there to protect you from this. "Have I taught you the things you need to be safe? What have I taught your brothers and sisters? The worst thing a dad can do sometimes is nothing. Sometimes he can't do anything at all.
I never thought that a member of our family could be a victim of a rape. I thought this happened to other people.

At first, I know you were hurt by so many people close to you that seemed to blame you. What were you wearing? Were you drinking? The people around you were angry and blamed you for your victimization. I, at first, blamed you also. How awful we were to you. The people who are supposed to love you. I pretended it didn't happen, I was helpless and you were spiraling downward.

I know this was not your fault. It is never the victim's fault. I wasn't there for you. I am sorry.

You had so many struggles in the aftermath of the rape. You describe that time as one of deep loneliness, feeling damaged and broken, not fully alive and scared.

You seemed so far away trapped in the horror of your experience. Just when I thought you had lost all hope, a friend stepped in and told you about the Victim Assistance Center. I remember how she held your hand and told you that help was just a phone call away.

On your first day at VAC, I was nervous and I know you were too. I remember when you left the house to go to your appointment; I could tell you were scared and embarrassed.

You took the risk to get help. Over time, I was humbled by your strength. Recovery was not always easy, but you allowed yourself to be vulnerable and open to change. You persevered in the face of adversity. You had setbacks and some very difficult periods but you started to heal.

You learned to make meaning out of your experience and rediscovered your precious self worth that was hidden for so long.

You are a true survivor and I love you.

Dad

(The above is a fictitious representation based upon real experience)

Sexual Assault is very real and is happening in our community.

Every 2 minutes someone in the United States is

sexually assaulted.

54% of sexual assaults are not reported to the police.

97% of rapists will never spend a day in jail.

66% of sexual assaults are committed by someone known to the victim.

93% of child sexual assault victims know their attacker.

Please support the Victim Assistance Center and the victims we serve. Thank you.

The Prostitute's Song

If you knew the years I spent,

trying to pull you out of my veins.

The blood lost- given- opening my arms and lying still.

Hoping your vapor would seek out the slits

you were so fond of and escape into the air.

Cause I always pictured you, your essence, wrapped

round me

Cat-like

woven through my nerves — burlap style.

I used to see you in the darkness,

your shadow creeping across my floor.

It became the thing lurking under my bed.

Hidden and grotesque and far more frightening

when I couldn't find it

than when I did.

I have grown used to paying for my life with my body.

I have grown tired

of paying for my life with my body.

It has always been my need,

to pay.

Broken bottles bite upon this bitter need to break,

to break.

To bury itself shoulder deep

and declare the world a war.

I am the Light, the Truth and the Way,

I am the cripple born on this day,

I am the apple that once fell from the tree,

I am the fallen, my Lord, glory be...

by Christine O'Leary-Rockey

The Power of "No"

I said,

you know,

we don't have to have sex.

He continued his quest

 for a condom

in the far reaches

 of the jungle in his closet.

Watching him look in every box,

under every shirt, on every shelf,

high and low

 I knew he was ashamed of sex.

Why else would he take such

precautions to hide a prophylactic?

He talked about Jesus as if his

purpose in dating me

was to bring me to Christ.

He talked about hanging out as if he

wanted to chat and watch movies, and

get to know me.

I should have known better, because

he talked about my butt

 as if I was not made of anything else,

as if I was not human like him.

No, I was just a body.

But I was lonely,

not yet proud of my big butt.

His compliments validated my yearning

 for some self-confidence.

I had waited years

to hear someone say that I look good.

I didn't need that.

What I needed was

to look in the mirror and

say, "Damn. I look good".

So, I found myself in his room,

enjoying some heavy petting.

I was waiting

 my turn to return the favor,

 when he went to the closet for a condom.

 I was relieved when

he didn't find it at first.

You know, we don't have to have sex,

I said.

Shouldn't that have been enough?

I said "don't", should I have used the

imperative mood instead?

Should I have shouted "no!"?

I knew I did not want him inside me.

He continued his quest for

a damn condom

in the far reaches

of the jungle in his closet.

I said,

You know, we don't have to have sex.

It wasn't violent, but

I did not want it and

I said the word "don't".

I have since learned the

power of the word, "no".

by Pam McMillin

Sister Midnight

I see Sister Midnight, Gena Olivier

Hauntingly beautiful

Smiling laughing

Singing dancing

All around

And I wonder

Clapping my hands

And my prick going whoop whoop

Remembering the Women of Bohemian

Chronicles of her "hood Glory days"

Greenwich Village

And Harlem

Particles of Love

Living in New York

With Andrea Barret

Smiling laughing

Singing dancing

With dadaíst Marcel Duchamps

Futurist Filippo Marinetti

And frightening forces of Nature

With exciting

Like the irresistible

Modernist Mina Loy

And the creative lunatic Baroness

Elsa von Freytay Loringhoven

Between curtain and glasses

And I wonder

I mean

Just being able

To pick and go.

by Daniel de Cullá

Humanity is Crying

Humanity is crying, yet the whole world ignores

The famine, the crimes, the massacres and wars

Truth is loud and clear but we shut our doors

Believing dishonorable media,

Supporting whoever pays more

Injustice and tyranny rise stepping upon nations,

Establishing merciless wicked legislations

Embedding poverty, destruction and starvation

All are done under the name of "civilization".

Men are wounded but fearless they stand,

To die in glory defending their land.

Babies breathe their last in mothers' hands

Irrigating with their precious blood the grass and sands.

Holding his tears remembering his father's last words,

"Don't grieve my death, be a fighter instead "

More wars are started seeking for diamonds and gold

Others most desire a blanket to shield em from the cold

Still eyes shut to the truth, to the lies we behold

Humanity is crying, still no answer?

The guilty commit crimes but the innocent are accused.

Girls, woman, little children are sexually abused

How can our minds still be confused?

Watching the corruption and villainy suffuse?

Every day, thousands die from sickness & starvation

Fortunes are spent on fur and leather to wear

Others are sleeping on the roads, cold and bare

Humanity is crying, longing to see the dawn

by Mahinour Tawfik

Ever Aftermath

1: The Marriage

When mother was dead, our father

finally asked my sister,

"Why didn't you tell me she was beating you?"

My sister responded:

"How could you not know?"

The king was in the counting house, doing his

accounting.

The king was buying his new Chrysler.

The king was drinking with his buddies,

fishing in his motorboat,

away on business, playing honky-tonk guitar

with his brothers in the den.

Taking his children, the mother fled into the forest

where a house made of gingerbread—

Wait. No. Those children were alone.

Taking the children she fled into a room where

a spinning wheel with a tainted spindle—

No, that can't be right.

Taking her children she fled into religion,

where she could pass them through a hole in god's

stomach

and drop them in the fire.

Taking the children she fled into a fury,

beat them with a belt, seized them by the ears,

banged their heads against a window pane.

The king said he did not realize

his wife was a witch who cast end spells

on his darling children

while he was busy looking the other way,

as, according to tradition, most men do.

2: Common Household Items Used against Children

apple

basket

beanstalk

birthday

braids

briars

cinders

cloak

frog

gingerbread

matches

mirror

oven

promise

rampion

riddle

rose

red shoes

spindle

splinter

words

by Carol Clark Williams

May Queen

They crowned her the queen of May,

the little girl.

Chose her for her purity.

Pure and white and smiling.

Unblooded.

Golden curls

held by red ribbons,

and entwined with flowers

topped with sweet smelling May.

Spring is here,

you see.

New shoots springing into life,

so we're ready to be

reborn and ready to play

the game.

Ready for the circle.

Ready to go

round and round again.

Like the dancers she watches

weaving their ribbons round

the Maypole.

The Maypole phallus they've planted

in the ground and

bedecked with ribbons.

Red and white.

Red and white ribbons of menstrual blood

and semen.

Round and round

She watches from her throne.

Round and round.

Then come the Morris Men.

Bells jangling their presence.

Sticks clashing with their power.

Flags waving

to announce

their virility.

They crowned her the queen of May,

the little girl.

A crown of sweet blossom

and hidden thorns.

by Lynn White

Exculpation

previously published in my book "Silence, Inhabited"
(NeoPoiesis Press)

Boy,

I see you:

once, I was you.

I cannot heal you.

(even if I could,

you are years away

from finding truth

in my admonitions).

Any connection I might make

would reveal in me the same lascivious light

that emanated from the tortured eyes

of he who first set me to howling –

any consolation I might afford

would diminish your capacity

to recognize future defilers,

impugning my higher purpose.

I can offer only this,

my indirect benediction...

You will soon begin a journey

(in truth, you have already begun).

You will never know your destination.

The map is a lie.

Everyone you meet will speak in riddles.

Those unlike you will not understand you,

nor will you understand them;

those like you will feast upon your affliction.

Rescuers with God in their eyes

will not prove equal

to the task of your redemption,

for they will not see

the mark of shame upon you;

well-meaning prophets of Baal

offer no comfort beyond now —

the time you lose in their embrace

can never be regained.

You will always blame yourself...

Your despoiler?

Fear him not;

he has forgotten you –

he is plowing fresher fields

(you have already yielded innocence,

which cannot be sown on the same ground twice).

Scavengers, whose heinous debauchery will follow

(sometimes at your request),

though their taloned scythes be just as sharp –

are merely demons

looming to vanish the instant you call them

by their rightful name.

Gradually,

you will purge your predilection

for the familiarity of their abominations.

Within you, a tarnished moral compass

flickers toward true North and hope;

though its magnetism will never again be immaculate,

still it will reckon, once you learn its terms...

Above all, your brokenness

must remain uncompromised;

its potency is the only insurance

against execrable perpetuation

of the horrors that have shaped you.

Your restlessness

heralds incipient manhood.

Go now,

but know:

this will never be finished.

Any faith you invest

in believing the curse can be reversed –

in believing the past can be forgotten –

is folly.

Your only achievable victory lies

in steadfast, righteous vigilance.

You must transmogrify

your lust for vengeance;

let grief engender a gyre of grace

lest humanity forsake you

'ere you receive Eleos' gifts

borne on the wings

of survival.

As a violin sings

only when bowed by its tormentor,

so must you scream honor

in the clutch of remembered evil...

Long after ghost fingers have ceased

their corrupt carnal caress,

one true chord will linger –

as its echoed anthem emerges,

your anguished ears will attune to the cry

of a waiting warrior.

Become that man.

Become a man

who could never do

what lesser men did

to the boy you were.

Become a man

who knows

that boy you were

can never be healed.

Become a man

who knows

that boy

can only be

forgiven.

by Rich Follett

The Web of Abuse

It is that spark of vulnerability; there is something that allows for the connection to happen, the meeting of the emotional stars. It may seem so satisfying and curious at first but it is more than anything you may have had before and maybe in some ways it is better. The intensity of it, the rush, the speed, the love-talk, the love act, doesn't it all happen so fast?

Within the speed is the dangerous whirl, that spinning vortex that before you can climb out of it you have begun to be sucked into it. It happens when you are so caught in the moment of the thrill and the chase that you do not see that the vortex is turning and you are yourself turning and turning. But what was it that drew you in? That spot, that place of vulnerability, that area in the heart that likes being flattered and charmed and made to feel that beautiful and important or valuable.

And before the vortex is done swirling you and around and whirling you into a powder, other things are entering in. The intensity of the vortex begins to have dark chakras, the energy goes sideways, the shock value begins to shock. *Am I different now that he is in my life? Did I do something wrong here? Is he just in a bad mood? Why do I get this feeling of foreboding? Why does this weird sense of fear come upon me? Of course it is just that this is so new and real and intense and wonderful, but why do I feel afraid somehow and why does part of me want to get away?*

That vortex entraps because of the speed at which it develops, and the less powerful nature of the object which gets caught within the whirl and swirl. The speed is a device and it can be a tool in the arsenal of the dominator seeking prey to dominate. Beware, oh deer in the headlights, for those pretty lights aiming into your eyes is the vortex coming to suck you in as you stare back unawares!

And so it starts this way. Within that whirl and swirl is some kind of pain, some kind of shock. You feel the nausea combined with dread. *Maybe I can't go on these kinds of rides, maybe I am not cut out for them, maybe I should try something else, or sit this out a while.* For a moment it slows and the nice energy returns and the nice strokes and pats return and the daisies in the field are under your feet again and the blues and whites of the princess and her long hair are dancing before your vision eyes again. *Perhaps I will get used to the speed of it, after all I just need some practice, perhaps maybe I caused the vortex to swing so hard around. I will go into the purple colors and swirl again.* Purple is the color of rich blood vessels when they are broken, but oh so pretty indeed a color it is, isn't it?

The vortex is a wheel, not the up and around of a Ferris wheel, but a sucking circling kind of wheel that spins and ignites from the energy that is in it, and that energy is you. Without you, the vortex would seek another energy, and with you, it becomes more alive and it swirls faster and you feel the swirl and it is fast, and exciting and a bit nauseating and a bit scary. In some ways it is better than the damp green grass of ordinary and fields of buttercups and daisies. And then the vortex shocks you once more, a little more of your energy is taken from you, you feel the depletion and yet you seem to stay. *But then should I get off? Can I get out?* But by the time you think again about it, the vortex has begin to embed itself into your legs and body, and you are embedded into it as well, those colors of purple and yellow and red, fire and bruised blood! And as you try to rid yourself of this vortex ride, behold! the sweet "sorries" come again; you hear the melodious strains of remorse, which sound as real as all the lute songs and trumpets in fairy land.

But mark me, the purples will come again against the fiery reds and yellows, the colors of anger and heat and the conversion of your energy into the vortex and those purples will even crack open to show the red from which they are truly made. Again and again and again and again and again.

The man in the middle of the vortex is the vortex itself, who both creates it and sustains himself by keeping you in it. Without you, the force would starve and grow angry. Then the force will cajole you back to itself with charms and potions that appeal to the heart. The thing that has grown from the two of you together is greater than the sum of your two parts. And without you upon which to feed and glean, the vortex will rise in greater fury to encapsulate you so that you cannot wrench your shoulder to be free or move your legs to run away. *The fairy land was in the vortex was it not, or was it? That dragon was not me, or him, was it?* You then belong to it. Do you accept this new identity? Do you think if you remain that all will be the goodness and nice energies again? Do you?

I know all these feelings and realities because I experienced them all. The whirlwind beginning, the state of vulnerability, the intensity of momentum so early on, getting into a ride that was going so fast I did not realize how far I was getting from the old world of normal until I was so enmeshed in it I found it hard to get away. My mind had already been altered to think differently, my ears had been acclimated to hearing cursing and put-downs, and eventually when the purple bruises came, I somehow thought I deserved them and that I made them happen somehow. And then when the red roses of repentance came in a bundle I would relent and return again. Eventually I returned even when there were no roses or even any "sorries" said to me any more at all.

But as the day rises and as the moon cycles through her phases, the cycle will continue and worsen unless you can heed the warning signs and get away and stay away. The warning signs were all there for me and I know I did not heed them. I spent half my life stuck and sucked in by the vortex. But even though it took me a long time I really did do it and I really am finally free. This is the future I want you to have, and I want you to have it sooner that I had it. So I wrote this book: *Warning Signs of Abuse: Get Out Early and Stay Free Forever*. I wrote it as a gift from my heart; learn from me, from where I went wrong and what I did right, so you have a chance to avoid my fate. Heed the warning signs of abuse, get out early and stay free forever!!!

by Theresa Rodriguez

The Predators

Her presence was sculpted

in his mind's black, dark cold.

Sick thoughts start to disperse,

that fuels the others,

like regiments carrying lanterns

lighting her every move.

She plays musical notes

that she knows not,

an unseen flute entwined

with infectious scents

egos fuelled by distracted glances

They seek out the note

that takes their crazed, crazed

Grand Canyon brush-stroke thoughts,

painting the night

in Lucifer's gallery's were angels

freeze in portraits long lost

to the one's

that were once blessed.

by Wayne Hislop

Anita's Dream

Anita's dream

of her Albuquerque

front lawn

and the bomb

of punching bags

fit round the side

used to flex some muscle

of the birth

of a song called Rumsfeld Blues

crooned to some girls sitting on used recliners

of the desert

without a grain of sand

sealed on the hearts, lips and minds

of Coyote Café kitchen workers

of Chihuahuas

who licked no one

save her owner and present narrator

of the next day

in bed when she let me touch her leg

before she concealed it like a switchblade

I didn't want to anyways

then over hair long and black

I tried on her buccaneer hat

still hiding in the corner

of barkeeps

that swoon

like Stevie Nicks

getting light-headed from elevation

of psychics

north of Santa Fe

who claim to have found

in ancient aeronautics

among the ethyrs

kind-of salvation

I can't say that I care

for this, or for anyone

but if the tribune gave the pope a thousand words

you deserve some.

by A. P. Lewis

That Guy

Statistics show now that 1 in 4 girls will be or have been

sexually assaulted

I'd like to say if I saw you again,

 that I would just walk right past

and pretend that I didn't see you trying to catch my eye

that I didn't have to still think of you as "that guy"

I would like to say that I would walk right up to you

and punch you in the face

I would sit back and yell

all about how much you are a fucking disgrace

I would scream at you

 "what the fuck and why? Why did you have to be that
guy?"

you took away the innocence

 the carefree me,

the one that played in pigtails and climbed up really tall
trees.

You took her heart away and locked her in the closest

So now at 26 I'm having a hard time trying to find it

I pray for the man who can undo what you have done.

But really and truly it can't be undone

the innocence is lost; the little girl has been finally freed

and now standing before me in the mirror,

is just plain ole me

The me that will have to shake the nightmares and
regrets

the me that will have to see that shadow of you

behind her at every turn

The me that will one day finally be able to let these
wounds

heal

The woman in me will understand

 that THAT was the BOY in you

But the little girl that had been trapped and stolen,

she will take longer to heal,

 but through kind words and prayers

she too will start to take flight

In all honesty,

I know that as time continues to pass and the scars
cease to grow,

That I would probably walk up and give you a hug,

hold you so tightly that you would think

that it was a sign from above,

to keep your eyes on the sky and keep walking in the
path of

Light

No sin or transgression no immoral delight

stays with this soul,

for it has been washed white

Rinsed anew in forgiveness until I am pure in Love's
sight

by Melisha Landreth

Threesome

I want to have a threesome

You, you and me

I want to see what is underneath

Not your skin or in these sheets

I want to know your darkest secrets

Your biggest fears highest dreams

I want you to bare your soul

bare it all to me

Allow me to be a testament for your divine

evolution

I don't want to be another problem but the

grander solution

I want to have a threesome

For both of you feel complete

I want to have a threesome

For I believe that is the true human feat

See we lie to ourselves

and only want to show ourselves to a few

but I ask myself why should I hold back for you?

Why can't I experience the presence

 of more than one at a time?

Why can't that be the true feminine divine?

I want to have a threesome

You you you you you you you you and me

Oh wait..

That's what we call a spiritual orgy

by Ed Go

Society's Problem Child

A child of nine

Seems to be

Between you and me

Emotionally

Disconnected.

Abandoned by mother

Father and his live-in on crack

Who don't give a jack

Lay a strap across his back

To make him harder.

Inner city

Born and raised

Never praised

A bullet grazed

Just yesterday.

His violent world

Filled with rage

At such a young age

It's hard to gauge

Should be protected.

Will the cycle ever end?

Has the youth any hope

But to end up on dope

Or at the end of a rope?

Society's problem

And society's child.

by Kenneth Vincent Walker

The Primal Scream

I'm reading "In Wintering:

A novel of Sylvia Plath"

By Kate Moses

Vividly recreating her vision

Of the final months

In the life of a doomed poet

During the winter of 1962

Into a final cycle of despair

That led to her

Exceptionally violent

Creepy suicide

Tracing the thread of my head

Into a web and so mysterious

Listening in the air

Courtney Love's

"America's Sweetheart"

Did you miss me, Courtney?

You have beautiful arches

And I orgasm very quickly

Dreaming of You

In the waves washing

The beaches of my mind

Perplexed, rocked

Seduced, overwhelmed

Baffled, irritated

And kicked in the ass

Spiriting as God

That sounds as if it has been

An intense time for You

Reprinted from Veins

In the perpetual

Weaving and reweaving

As V.K. McCarty says:

"The primal scream, I hear it

And I really 'feel'

Sylvia Plath

When She fell

Like a signal:

Of ourselves

by Daniel de Cullá

The Smell of Lilac

As I lie in bed starring at the ceiling I can hear Aunt Sandy in the kitchen. I know her every move just from the various sounds in the house. Six a.m., the squeak of the front door that needs badly oiled. She is going out to get the daily newspaper. The scrape of the kitchen chair against the worn floral patterned linoleum and the crinkling of the paper as she sits to look for coupons and yard sales.

Seven a.m.

Creak creakcreakcreak, as she heads back upstairs for her shower. The smell of lilac soap seeps into every room of the tiny house. It breaches the door of my tiny room. Assaults my nose. Over powers the scent of the early morning breeze that had only moments ago found its way into my window. I feel as if I will be chocked by the sickeningly sweet stench of it.
Creak creakcrakcreak, water running now the faint lilac is overpowered by the dark smells of freshly ground coffee beans roasting.

Clanging now as pans are put on the stove. I hear the sizzle of the bacon before I can even smell it. My stomach clenches. I know it is almost eight am and that soon Aunt Sandy will be coming to get me up. For a moment I imagine the weak limp uncooked bacon in the pan. Imagine myself as the strong sizzle with the power to burn, to take control of the situation and shrink those that try to infiltrate me.
It only lasts a moment. I know that I am the limp bacon.

Eight a.m.

I squeeze my eyes shut and pretend to be asleep as she enters the room. I hear the splash of the water as she fills the basin beside the bed with steamy hot water. Hear the wrapper on the fresh bar of lilac soap she opens and places beside the basin. I can smell it now. I hate that smell "Emily, honey. Time to get up and get the day started."

I open my eyes; she is leaning over me, sweet loving smile on her face. Aunt Sandy kisses me on the cheek. Her breath smells like stale cigarette, coffee and brandy or whatever she had sipped on this morning. Her skin smells of lilac.

"Good morning Aunt Sandy."

I hate her. I love her. Nobody else cares if I live or die. I'm not even sure if I care. But she seems sure that she cares. Why else would she let me live here with her? Why else would she take care of me?

"Ok, let's get you cleaned up. Just because we have no place to go today doesn't mean we just lay in bed all day long." She raised the bed to a level where she wouldn't have to bend as far. "Let's sit you up so that we can get this nightgown off of you. " Aunt Sandy took my hands and helped me to a semi sitting position. Once she was sure that I was steady she reached beneath me to grab the end of the nightgown and pull it up to my waist. I was then able to pull my arms out and take it over my head. I was completely nude and completely embarrassed. It always made me feel embarrassed to be nude in front of Aunt Sandy. For the last three years this had been the daily routine and for the last three years I was embarrassed each time.

She first gave me my toothbrush, tooth paste already on it and placed on hand on my back to balance me while I brushed me teeth. With her other hand she held a cup for me to rinse then spit into. Brush, rinse, spit. She put the cup down and gave me the second cup she had by the bedside. The foul taste of Listerine entered my mouth, burned my nose. Rinse, spit. I glanced down at my legs. Useless. I had no feeling in them at all. They had become shriveled with lack of exercise. They were now the enemy, fighting against me and my desire to leave my aunt's house. The enemy that will not allow me to kick, clench or runaway. I hate my legs.

Eight fifteen.

The water in the basin has cooled a bit. The steam is no longer rising like smoke from an angry volcano, but has become wisps slowly falling over the rim of the basin. Eight twenty. This is the part I had been dreading, the part that made small beads of sweat breakout on my forehead, the only outward sign of fear I could not stop from showing.

Aunt Sandy gently put her hands on my hips and slid me back down to lay flat on my back. Then reaching into the bedside table she pulled out a clean washcloth. I watched her; however she never looked me in the eye, just went about her chore of preparing to bathe me. I could tell what kind of day it would be by what supplies she pulled from the drawers. So far just a washcloth. Maybe she was in a hurry today and she would bathe me quickly and go about her day.

No, it was just wishful thinking. Aunt Sandy continued to rummage in the rickety old side table pulling out first cotton swabs, then scissors and finally the Vaseline. I turn my head away, stomach churning again. I lie there starring at the ceiling.

Eight twenty-two.

Aunt Sandy begins to hum. Something sounding a bit like what I could only think was an attempt at something soothing. To me it was only setting the scene before Jekyll turns into Hyde.

"Arms out." She says.

I obey without question. I had stopped questioning a long time ago. I lie there crucifixion-style, naked. She dips the washcloth in the warm water. I smell the lilac as she soaps the cloth. Feel the bile reach the top of my throat. She starts with my arms, running the soapy cloth over them.

Eight twenty-five.

My armpits, my hands. Dips the cloth in the water, soap the cloth, now my neck and chest.

Eight thirty.

Dip the cloth, soap the cloth. She lefts first my left breast, slowly soaping in slow circles, then the right breast.

I pretend it's not happening. I can hear the traffic outside. Horns blare in the background, birds chirp in the tree outside of my window. I am not here in this stuffy little room. I am not here.

Eight forty-five.

Dip the cloth, soap the cloth, slow soapy circles on my stomach, my side. Dip the cloth, soap the cloth.
Now she is at the bottom of the bed, I know that she is adding the same soapy circles to my feet and legs. I feel the sweat beads start to roll down my face.

I can't help it, I glance at the mirror that hangs on the closet. My room is a tiny shoebox in the corner of the house. It looks much the same as it did when I spent summers here as a small child. Dolls still align the shelves along with tattered copies of The Three Little Kitten, Aesop's Fables and other early readings. The blue wallpaper has long faded to a lighter shade. The old wood floor, which is polished weekly still shines at the spots where it peeks from beneath the braided circular rug.

Aunt sandy has an almost stone-like look on her face as she moves the washcloth up and down my now spread legs. I look away, I don't want to see this, don't want to be here with these legs that don't run. I feel the warm cloth on my vagina.

Slow soapy circles, she lingers there.

Nine a.m.

I shut my eyes tight as my aunt takes the water basin to replace the soapy lilac scented water with fresh water to rinse with. Am I breathing? I am not sure.

Back with the clean water Aunt Sandy repeats the process all over again. Dip cloth, rinse, dip, left breast, right breast, legs. Vagina. Linger. She takes a cotton swab, dip. She runs the tip over my clitoris, around my clitoris. I'm not here.

I am at school. Track practice. Running, running till my chest is tight and the wind rubs my face. I am running into the wind forcing myself to fight against it. The wind is never at my back. I am strong and fast as the world turns to a blur.

I'm not here.

"We want to make sure everything is clean, women are prone to infection and all sorts of things like that. I won't have anyone saying I have not been taking proper care of you." All this said as the swab continues its path around my clitoris.

I wonder if she imagines it as a train going around a track.

Circle, circle circle. My stomach churns and clenches.

Nine twenty. The train finally stops. I hear her get the scissors. Snip. Snip snipsnip snip. She keeps me trimmed, very trimmed. Warm wash cloth making circles on my freshly clipped pubic area.

"There you go, all clean and fresh." I could feel my face flush as aunt sandy eyed my naked body. "You know, I was your age once."

I continued to stare at the ceiling as she opened the Vaseline.

I could hear her rubbing it on her hands, the slight smell of it mingling with the soap.

"I had needs at your age. Perfectly natural needs. You're lucky I understand about these things and that am here to help you."

Nine forty.

I could feel her invade my vagina with her fingers. Forcing her way in as she continued talking. Feel the one and only tear I would shed today slide down my cheek. She keeps talking as she pushes her fingers in and out of me. Reassuring me that this was to help me so that I would not feel soo "frustrated".
I try to get lost in the world outside, listen for the horns, the birds, anything. All I can hear is Aunt Sandy's sing-song voice and my own chocked breathing. I can't escape.

Ten a.m.

I am in a fresh new nightgown. Aunt Sandy kisses me again. On the lips this time. Quickly. But not soo quick that I cannot feel the chapped skin against my own. Her skin smells of lilac, my skin smells of lilac.

I hate Aunt Sandy. She must love me right?
I love Aunt Sandy; she takes very good care of me.

by T.L. Waid

La Belle Dame Sans Merci

Fumbled affairs and Internet fucks

Thanking the almighty penis for restoring our

fleshly selves

to Godliness...

Ladies, we've got to do better than this.

Painting, always painting, the disguise of

ourselves

Going blond as we chase that pointy-breasted

svelte and always Starving

image of ourselves that we never were.

Insisting that all women remain seventeen...

Ladies, we gotta do better than this.

Living off of men and comparing the size of his

dong

The devoted pursuit of the perfect outfit/the

Highest heel/the biggest rock-
The length of our nails gone three inches long we

are like

Peacocks gone wild...

Dumbed down and dirty,

Whether pavement brawls or board-room fucks-
All for the right to say — look what I got

It makes me what I am.

Ladies. We GOTTA do better than this.

Waiting for a prince to give you the roll of your

life

No matter how crazed, how cruel, how vain you

get

A corporate bitch sucking off his credit cards

With two sets of red lips and a brain just the

right size

For a homicide.

Then crumble like a doll when he's off with the

next Cruella

With a tighter ass...

Ladies we oughta be better than this.

The Lady, always the Lady

You who never bends, never ruffles, never threw

A damned thing just stood there patiently-

always the lady- always

The cross, willing to sacrifice yourself and your

children

To the great god of silence...

Your silence breeds rape and basement incest

The simmering pestilence of the unseen, call it

tacit compliance

Your momma never said a word and neither will

You

Cause you were just a whore

all along — she said so,

or so you think, so he told you

when he spent his corruption

Into your ear.

Your thighs just happened to be there...

When did we become voiceless like worms —

was it when they killed off our gods?

Changed Isis for Mary and Jesus

For Paul?

Now we are our own best assassins — cutting

off the noses

the frontal lobes

Of the women who would restore us

and handing our daughters the keys

to our own therapeutic needs

To capitulate. We teach them

to capitulate,

And turn to the men

to redeem us.

by Christine O'Leary-Rockey

The Liar

As you leave, all your lies

Drag in your wake

Like tin cans

Tied to a

Newly wed's car

I wish I knew

I wish I knew

The way to the door.

The windows are for

Looking out during storms.

With a door I could leave.

With a window

I can only

See myself coming.

by Sandi Leonard Polvinale

Saturday Nights

The clues always surface sometime pass six

freedom rock echoes from the garage

right foot shuffles on the stone driveway

blotchy red face

jutted chin

we can smell fear

he and I

it burrows in

affixed to the farm to me

and it compliments his swift swagger

she hides in the house

cleaning the kitchen

over and over

and cooks my favorite meal

hoping to loosen my locked jaw.

by Kara Valore

Moments for Liana

"*People who truly love only know moments*"

she shared my love of love

and my penchant for la gaudier

we both knew that I couldn't believe her

when she called me beautiful

we both knew that we didn't believe each other

when we listed our reasons for holding on

despite the broken horror

pieces that we'd let ourselves become

I knew that I had to love her

and she had to love me

as I told her the story

of a mind raped to rapture

and the rabbit hole trap door

that I jumped in long ago

I could feel him bandaging

my ravaged wrists, his heart

showing with the salve

but it was her voice that I heard

her melancholy

that he had been lucky enough

to love me that way

whilst she was still lost in

hoping to be needed

"I would've loved you for a million years"

it sounded like a plea

and after I kissed her good night

it occurred to me that I forgot to tell her

I would have let her

by Missi McLaren Ritter

The Hour Glass

Previously published

They once lived in a house of refined glass

That was tormented by a slurring wind

That kissed and spat and smashed.

The pursuing harsh bitter wind

Showed its toll.

As the glass received chips,

Then shattered, it had long reformed

To sand; there was no sparkle of life

Not even a movement or a ripple,

The dance ceased.

A battle was once fought here –

No winner or loser

But never the less

There was no more distress

No SOS

In this sand, that once

resembled a stain of glass

that captured a ray of light

on a reflection of a more composed time

Now forgotten.

by Wayne Hislop

Your Pain, My Heart

I wrote your pain

on my heart,

there,

a heart.

Passed my skin

through my rib cage

into my flesh,

a heart.

Those pains which you have

suffered,

your past,

my future.

Your wounds

hurt,

you tried to cover them but

the dressings

didn't fit.

You are no healer.

Those wounds scar me,

your wounds,

so I inked them into my

skin.

My

self.

My body.

Anybody can see,

except you.

I cried for you: once

For myself: never

I cried when

I fell out of love

(Have you ever fallen?

It hurts)

Have you ever felt hurt?

I heard that you had,

but you have forgotten.

by Pam McMillin

Jennifer's Story

It was the fall of 2005 and nine-months had gone by. It was time for Ray's ship to arrive from deployment. I had flown down to California for the homecoming. I was 19, so excited to see him and had planned a wonderful vacation for the two of us. From the time Ray walked off the aircraft carrier, I could sense there was something wrong. When we found each other in the crowd, he barely kissed me. He didn't compliment me on the outfit I wore or thank me for coming. Ray appeared anxious, short tempered and his comments were sarcastic.

After staying overnight in San Diego, we headed to Las Vegas. Wanting to help Ray relax while providing a romantic atmosphere, I had booked a room with a king size bed and Jacuzzi. It was expensive but I felt we were worth it. During our stay, Ray didn't show any interest in being intimate with me anymore. After a long deployment, I expected him to be affectionate upon his return home to me. I expected him to want sex. Now the tables had turned and I had to initiate sex. Reluctantly, he would comply but it felt forced on his part, which never used to be the case. This behavior raised questions. Although I didn't have proof, Ray was showing all the signs of someone who was being unfaithful. To make matters worse, once he gambled all of his money away, he quickly tried to drain me of mine.

Before I knew it, I was trying to raise my credit limit to keep us both afloat. Our nice getaway became a personal nightmare for me. I couldn't put my finger on it, but Ray had really changed for the worst.

Once we returned back home, Ray complained how he didn't have any friends and that a few of his co-workers from his squadron were meeting at the Chief's Club. I had no issue with this and supported his desire to make friends. Wanting him to be safe while drinking, I volunteered to be his designated driver and dropped him off. By midnight, he had not called for me to pick him up nor called to say he was ok. Worried, I jumped in my car, still wearing my pajamas, and went to look for him. He was not where I had dropped him off. I drove around for a while searching for him. But he was nowhere to be found. Concerned and anxious, but not knowing where else to look, I went home and waited for him. Later, in the early morning hours, he finally showed up on our doorstep ringing the doorbell to be let in. He was drunk as a skunk!

Additionally, Ray offered no excuse as to why he was out all night long without calling. Nor did it cross his mind that I would be concerned for his safety. It didn't even occur to him that as only a "girlfriend" and not a "wife" the police or hospital staff would not be as forthcoming in giving me information had he ended up in one of those places.

After all my years taking his crap and remaining devoted, this was the ultimate slap in the face. I couldn't continue on this path. I deserved better. I also knew that I was at my breaking point with his disrespect, abusive ways and now potential infidelity. How dare he do this to me!

So often at night I would lie awake pissed off. It blew my mind how he could sleep so peacefully without a care in the world. I cried so much that my tears stained my pillowcase. Although I tried to muffle the sounds of my crying, I knew Ray heard me. He ignored me and pretended to sleep. He gave me the cold shoulder and my feelings were hurt. Ray just didn't care. Upset, I would turn and glare at him as I thought of putting a pillow over his head and taking his life. Even though I wanted to hurt him I recognized that Ray was not worth me going to jail. Clearly, this is not healthy and something had to give.

His behavior while intoxicated was embarrassing and the name-calling was out of control and humiliating.

According to Ray, I wasn't good enough and he made it his business to tell me so. How could someone who professed their love for me continually point out every flaw that I was self-conscious about? A new year was approaching and I refused to be his physical, emotional and verbal punching bag. I deserved better but wasn't sure how to get on the path of healing. Finally, I grew tired of unanswered phone calls, unexplained phone numbers in the pocket, broken promises, sexual dissatisfaction, uncontrolled finances, loneliness and depression. I knew a change had to come.

Through going to church, renewing my relationship with the Lord and, of course, listening to many Mary J. Blige songs, I began to find strength, peace and joy that I hadn't had in quite some time. I needed to refocus on what was important: Me. I had a desire to become whole again, mind, body and spirit. It wasn't necessary for me to rush home, especially when Ray was still on a mini deployment late 2005. While he was away my confidence continued to grow. Mentally and emotionally I became stronger.

It was approaching 2006 and with a new year, I was determined to make it my new beginning. No more foolishness from Ray and having low self-esteem. I was done drowning in my tears or giving my all to someone who didn't deserve it. I wanted to leave but knew our lease wouldn't be up for another six months. I felt stuck.

One morning while getting ready for work, I poured my heart out to the Lord. I prayed for wisdom, clarity and strength to escape this relationship. It was like a light bulb came over my head with the answers. I felt

God's presence. I followed God's directions and when things started in motion there was no time to turn back.

At the first opportunity, I went to the property management office to talk to the ladies to whom we paid our monthly rent. I told them my dilemma of needing to move and start fresh but I didn't want to lose my deposit for breaking the current lease. The ladies understood and told me that they had an apartment I might be interested in. There was an apartment in the downtown area that they hadn't advertised yet and would also be willing to reduce the rent for me. Not only were they willing to do that, but they would also let me out of our lease and use the deposit towards the new apartment.

Those ladies actually stopped what they were doing, hopped in a car and took me to see the apartment. I followed God's direction. When I tell you God was putting things in motion, He was! Things were moving so fast I didn't have time to hesitate or back pedal.

Fed up and ready to move on, by mid-January 2006, I told Ray it was over and that I had enough of him being inconsiderate. I was emotionally depleted from him treating me like garbage and taking advantage of me. Of course he began to cry and didn't want things to end. I told him he could have everything I bought in the sports room. I didn't want much and wasn't in the mood to argue about who gets what. I wanted my freedom. He became worried about where he would live and, like a good person, I told him the ladies at the rental office had a few places available he might be able to afford.

Going our separate ways was not easy for me. In the first place, five and half years is a lot of time to invest in a person and then have to walk away. I didn't think I had the courage to be without Ray. Second, there were some good memories. I held out hope, thinking things would change for the better. I wanted so badly to get married and have children with him. I figured if I loved harder and stronger, he would see that I was the one for him. It was natural for me to see the best in everyone and Ray was no different. Additionally, I didn't want to admit to myself that I had stayed with someone who was abusive.

I had to swallow my pride after wearing a smile on my face for so long. The last thing I wanted to do was acknowledge I had gotten it wrong again. I was sure I had learned my lesson and knew better. I was disappointed in myself for not following my intuition at the first sign of trouble. Lastly, I was emotionally exhausted with low self-esteem. I was afraid that no one would want me. Being the kind-hearted person I am, I sometimes felt guilty for hurting his feelings by leaving him. I was still putting my feelings last. Nevertheless, I recognized that breaking up with Ray and moving forward was necessary in order to properly treat my wounds.

Due to shame and wanting to avoid conflict, I kept my abuse from family and friends. I especially didn't want them to be upset and go after Ray. Still, I stepped out on faith and even though it showed I was vulnerable, I shared what I had been going through. I felt extremely blessed to have had the support from so many family and friends. Not once did they judge or talk down to me.

They gave me a place to stay, helped me pack and moved my belongings into my new apartment.
Despite all the love and support I had received, I still felt embarrassed and alone. However, as I continued to open up and share, other women came forward. What I found out was that I wasn't alone. I drew strength from every woman who related and shared their story too.

Looking back on our relationship, I recognize and thank God for knowing what was best for me. The philosophy that "time heals all wounds" is true. I knew something had to change. In order for that change to happen, I needed to be honest with myself and once again take a personal inventory. Although it was hard to swallow, I realized that I was the common denominator to my many disappointments. I didn't set my standards high enough and I lost sight of the fact that the love I was looking for needed to start with me.

Reevaluating my priorities again, I acknowledged that I needed to love and value myself first. Until I could do that, how could I expect someone else to do the same? I was trying to be superwoman to guys who were not ready to be with a woman like me. Instead of trying to change them, I was the one that needed changing. I couldn't control the behaviors of those men but I sure could control my behavior. I drew closer and strengthened my relationship with my Lord and Savior Jesus Christ, and rebuilt my self-esteem. I went back to using the affirmations that had worked in unacceptable relationships in my past. Every day when I got up, I would look in the mirror and say something positive about myself. I knew that when the time presented itself, I would approach my next relationship differently.

Being sick and tired of being sick and tired led to insight and a necessary transformation. When I got tired of the same results, which played like a continuous loop, that's when change happened. Change is not pretty, comfortable, easy or fast. But for my personal growth and development it was essential to achieving a quality of life I knew I deserved. As time went on, that gash turned into a scar. It became my beauty scar of survival.

by Jennifer C. Foxworthy

Midnight Ramblings

Where do I run to

When the one I love is the one chasing me?

How do I find protection and comfort

When the one I run to is the one I need protection from?

How do I find peace and resolution

When he feels he is justified in his actions?

How do I stay

When I'm running against insurmountable odds?

How do I go

When he's my existence?

by Gale L. Sherrid

Fish Tales and Sodomy and other Forms of Chivalry

You had a good girl and were fascinated

By the promiscuity she began to exhibit in the bar.

Willing to do things with others watching

While she drank herself under a table....

Rule 1:

If a woman says no she means it.

They never mean it, you say

And enjoy it rough

But if you say so, you say laughing...

For all of those girls out there who come back for more

For all of those girls in their party clothes and

Zealous breasts, giving you thigh and crotch shot for one

Casual thought and maybe

A night.

Rule 2. You can be a gentleman without being a wimp

Your sexual liberation rings horribly of sadism

She's giving it to guys now in the bar

Baby, you've really loosened up lately —

So come over here and do me again

Before I throw you back to the dogs.

Is she obedient? Or do you throw her down if she balks-

Pinning her with your weight and your perfect

Aim- I never hit a woman you say

And you don't.

Rule 3:

Try to think of a woman as something other than a

pussy with legs...

The army taught you to marry a skinny girl

So the weight she gained would curve and not

Drown her. That is your job

That and starvation- basic training of the psyche

Teaching her to love the iron butterfly and perform

Just for you

And your friends.

Shut up baby- just shut up- I ain't done yet

And you're getting on my nerves.

It's a victory to know that you fucked so hard I bled.

You're laughing and say

You're gonna tell your friends about it at the bar next

time,

Like recounting a fish tale that never needs to get

 bigger.

But it's your innocence that makes it all so real....

Rule 4

Treat a woman the way that you want someone to treat

your daughter

For most women, opening the legs

Is opening herself

And she is inviting you in.

And while you'd never dream of breaking into a man's

house

And running amok, smashing pictures and

Furniture,

Every invasion is a greater death

Till the things that once delicately held her together

Are replaced by you and your casual brutality.

It's the burglary that never ends.

It's not just the break-in that leaves you violated-

But the smashing through your intimate life

Without even thinking twice.

You can live without the money-

But you will never feel safe

Again.

Rule 5:

A woman is a human being the way that you are a

human being.

A man like you

Finds no pride in wounding a small thing,

Fighting a weak thing,

Or breaking the already broke.

And I've seen you walk away from more fights

Cause they were too drunk to know

That you would wipe them out clean...

Two shots- then go away

Before I have to hurt you

You'd say...

Rule 6:

And above all else- the mantra is: To do no harm....

by Christine O'Leary-Rockey

The Page

Nitrous patrols in poised positioned

Isles, lobed glares

Distorting my space

In regular targeting rounds

The boom rabidly intensifies

Yet again!

In the classroom the teacher looms

Shuttle breaths whisper

Harshly to my left ear

"Waste of paper and ink for you my son".

The eliminator I mean the educator herds

The strong writers and sophisticated voices now his

Reliable friends

My struggling education 'A' and 'The'

My only friends but sometimes more

And my pen freezes and my mind shatters the biro

As unseen cloud clash,

Above my head colossal words start to assemble

With thunderous words raging raging

But don't spill to an almost empty page.

Just a signed and dated name with my own reliable

friends

by Wayne Hislop

Once He was My Love

I can't tell you a story- I can only tell you part of a story-
because I never know where to begin. See each of our
lives is a story- only we don't know it, see? We know,
while watching a movie, that there is more to come. that
the characters will change. that some bad ass stuff
might happen. We know there'll be struggle, we know
there'll be hurt. We know that the lead role might even
get her ass handed to her at one point. Maybe two. but
what we don't know —often never think of- is that we are
in the middle of our own story.

I can't tell you how this begins. I can only tell you
where it ends. where it ended. And it never ended. not
really. if it had, I wouldn't be here telling you this...

So I'm on the phone with him- shit head, that is. My
rapist. Once he was my love. or at least my lover- and
that is where I became confused. See, he never hit me.
He never screamed at me. He never pushed me into
walls- only floors. or beds. Once in a while, a couch. And
see- I was used to being hit. I had been hit so often
when I was a kid- I knew I would never be hit again. I
knew that if he hit me I'd have been out of there. I'd
have been gone...but he never hit me. And therein, I
never knew...

And they're so good at making you think it's your
fault. 'I wouldn't have had to do that if you'd have shut
up'. 'shut up woman- it's not going to kill you'. 'Shut up-
just shut up- I'm not done with you yet, and you're
getting on my nerves...' and see, that's what you hear.
That's the tape that plays over and over in your head,

long after the rape- or rapes- are done. Those are the words that overplay, while you turn them over in your mind- usually just as flashes. Images that are out of order, that are random. Memories that come up at the oddest of times and sometimes you're not even sure if they are. Memories, that is...what if you imagined them?

What if it really wasn't that bad- what if you're exaggerating it? Misquoting it? What if it really was you all of the while?

So anyway, I'm on the phone with him and he's telling me about his new girlfriend- a super-cool chick who used to be really goody-goody and uptight. She's really loosened up, he tells me. When she's drunk she'll even give me a blowjob in the bar, under the table, in front of my friends...

'Dude- that's not cool. That's damage', I tell him. You need to know that. If this is a whole new behavior- if she's behaving like that now- and she wasn't like that before you- dude- that's damage.' You gotta know you're beating her down...

He laughs. I hear him laugh over the phone and just want to smack him- I'm half sick. 'Bull shit', he says. No one's making her stay around...but if you say so, baby...if you say so- you say. 'So why don't you tell me the rules....'

<read poem: *Fish Tales and Sodomy, and Other Forms of Chivalry*>

see- here's the thing:

This is a story. It's a part of a story. Once upon a time; one day in the rain, In the beginning there was only water. Once there was only water. In the beginning, there was only water, and God's breath blew across the face of the sea...

And you're like that too. Inside of a story. And it's you're in your own story. You're the hero of it- the main character- and maybe you're in the middle of getting beaten down...but think about it: We've all seen this part of the story...

The hero is down. S/he's getting beaten by the bad guy...after all of the struggle and amazing fight, you see the part where the hero looks like s/he's finally gonna go down...

What happens next? I'm asking you- what's the next part of the show?

C'mon- you've all seen this movie...

Just when it's darkest, when it seems all is lost and so don't know how they'll ever survive- it happens. A side-swipe. A lucky blow, a pivotal choice and the hero breaks free. Bloody, broken, often she's bleeding profound- but she rises. Somehow, some way she realizes that there's only one way to win this fight- only one real way to survive...

And that's by getting up. By fighting back. by refusing to quit, by refusing to ever stay down...

And that's my story. And it's your story. This is YOUR story. Your story. And you're in the midst of it- and maybe you're in the place where you're getting your ass handed to you, maybe you can't see anything but down...

But you're story isn't finished, this isn't over- even if you're in the midst of going down....

There is no ultimate battle. Only skirmishes, localized fights. In the end, the fight is only ended, the hero only triumphs, when they finally and truly refuse to stay down. And we all know this doesn't happen at the end of the movie- it's the middle.

It's the moment the hero finally resolves to survive....

So do it. and if you're afraid, do it anyway. Do it knowing that they only way to do it- do anything- is to get back up, realizing that the fight you're in is important.

That it will determine the fate of the world...

You didn't realize you were so important, did you?

by Christine O'Leary-Rockey

Oral History

How strange to smash the places that you kiss

as my father fist smashed my mother's lips.

If asked about her scars, she laughed and said

she slipped and fell face first against the tracks

on Railroad Street. Her marriage was a face-first fall

along the wrong side of the tracks.

There are paring knives in every kitchen drawer

curved to be cradled in a woman's palm.

She'd pause, weapon in hand over the stove,

then turn the knife against the vegetables.

From her scarred lips came words that slipped

like knives beneath a child's soft skin;

iron words, pointed and blunt like railroad spikes

to pin our small souls down.

Once in the hospital for some accidental injury

like childbirth, or a beating,

my mother was told by a nurse

that a man's hand is sensitive,

the palm so full of nerve endings, a slap can be

an act of love like a kiss. A nurse said this.

They are all dead now. Death can be an act of love.

In some countries witch doctors sew crossed strips

of rawhide over the corpse's eyes,

then seal the cold lips with a running stitch.

Strange custom, among strangers.

Perhaps better to seal the mouth at birth—

her lips or ours—over the sullen scars.

How strange to smash the people that you kiss.

by Carol Clark Williams

She Traded Old Rooms for a Determined Escape

Her bedroom was a shrewd junk dealer

worked from each end and met in the middle

Not bad, of course, compared to the other rooms

she was told were open to her,

although it doesn't have heat some days

and even in summer, feels cold

A go between you know, that bed was,

and a long trip made longer,

still holding the scent of some friends, her mother, other

young Black girls,

a paradise market filled with the aroma of the

showroom

After years, finally paid for - she was a used toy

a mere transaction at a 40 percent commission turn

around,

the provision that each bee bring some honey of his own

Take your time girl,

you're a washed and polished windshield

pulled out of a paper wrap, nice and

"practically new"

penciled on the bag

This house doesn't own you

and your sturdy body still has years of strength

and use left in it.

You can trade this room

for a determined escape.

And she did.

by Carla Christopher-Waid

Tinsel and Tonsils

wretched and wrecked

ruined my best dress

to label my vials of vomit

for the numbered days of April

and of him and I

learning that ends don't meet

and beginnings are like toothbrushes

loyal to the throat

until one day

your gag reflex walks out on you

defeated and angry

by Missi McLaren Ritter

It's Time to Speak Out

I've spent the last three years in silence-keeping secrets, sweeping things under the rug, living a lie. I finally refused to continue to minimize what has happened to me. When is it ok for a man to put his hands on a woman? To what extent can anyone justify causing harm to someone who is much smaller and weaker than they are? I have been living a cliché by justifying every action, blaming myself, and denying what this truly was. The bottom line is it is NEVER ok for a man to physically harm a woman. Looking from the outside in it is so easy to grasp that, but I lived on the inside where I was constantly made to feel like it was my fault. I was threatened and provoked with harsh and demeaning words. I was quietly controlled and isolated with manipulations. I was antagonized and set up by being recorded with a camera phone when I would hit my emotional limit.

The lies and manipulations worked, I am sad to admit. I watched my friends and family slowly leave my side as I was made to believe that they were the enemies. I stopped enjoying things I would normally enjoy because I felt guilty. I put to the side one of my greatest passions- my music. I became controlling in the relationship because I didn't feel in control of my life anymore. I basically enabled the abuse to escalate until... the excuses ran out.

When you fear for your life for an hour and a half straight, it does something to the love you once felt for the person who is sitting on top of you with his hands around your neck.

When your life is flashing before your eyes, suddenly life on your own seems to be better than life with this person who has lost all control and is now foaming at the mouth. I can speculate all I'd like as to why a person would abuse someone they proclaim to love so much. Maybe it's their own abusive childhood, maybe it's a mental or personality disorder, or maybe its drug and alcohol induced behavior. Of course to the abuser these fits of rage have been brought on by something the victim has done. I've been accused of cheating, which breaks my heart because that couldn't have been further from my mind.

I guess I nagged too much about receiving money so that I could pay the bills on time. I suppose it wasn't fair for me to expect someone who is working from home all day to help out around the house a little bit more. Maybe I shouldn't have hid the alcohol or poured out his glass when he had too much. It's not in my nature to back down from an argument, but I learned real fast that being confrontational was a mistake. Sure I would stomp my foot, yell, and cry hysterically when he would try to flatten me out with his sharp words and then literally close the door in my face. He would threaten to leave and sometimes he would and I'd have no idea where he had gone until the next day. Sometimes I'd follow him, my mind too foggy to think rationally. After a while I stopped chasing and pleading for him to listen to me. I felt trapped. I started to pack my stuff and leave when he would go off on his hurtful tangents and I'd feel my blood begin to boil.

I soon found that leaving only triggered the abuse more. I'd come home and he was just waiting to unleash everything that was bottled up from the time I walked out the door. I can overanalyze everything that I may have done wrong in the relationship, but the reason for the abuse doesn't really matter. Any rational person knows that. I needed to be safe and get the hell out. As I began to read the literature on leaving an abusive relationship, it was clear that the abuse would most likely escalate and it would be extremely difficult for me to leave. Let me tell you from experience and without a doubt, it would've been easier to stay. I suddenly empathized with all of those women who have never left their abusers. It had been going on three years and I was still here? Who had I become? Why was I constantly defending him and our relationship to everyone around me? Even his best friend was telling me to run for the hills. It was time.

They say 20/20 is hindsight. I think they say that so you don't feel like a complete idiot for making really bad decisions. Maybe I'm not believable because I continued to love him unconditionally. After all, I never filed any police reports after feeling like I'd been hit by a truck. I remember going into work with my bruises mostly covered, my throat sore from being choked, little or no sleep, sometimes limping, and just trying to smile through the physical and emotional pain and make it through the day. Why didn't I do anything? I don't know quite how to explain the utter confusion you feel when the person you're in love with is hurting you. I suppose I split him into two different people.

I longed for the man I fell in love with, my "soulmate," but feared the man that would resurface time and time again. The emotional conflicts I continue to struggle with after leaving someone I cared so much about and shared so much intimacy and passion with are only part of the aftermath.

I had gained a stepson through this relationship. I parented that child with all my heart. Even though my parenting skills weren't well received or appreciated fully, I did the best for that kid. I know it, he knows it, and I hope he will never forget those three years of complete devotion and normalcy. My heart cries for him. My son, who is ultimately my only responsibility, cried for him too. There was nothing more I could do for him without compromising my own safety and that of my child's. That's where a mother draws the line. I did what I had to do, but I miss that kid.

The kids were definitely a big reason why I stayed as long as I did. I remember working through escape plans in my head and the end result was always the same- what about the boys? Once I realized that my life was literally at stake I decided I had no choice but to leave. All the literature in the world couldn't really prepare me for what was about to happen next. I knew he wasn't going to take me leaving very well at all, but losing control was more than he could handle.

At first I had to deal with incessant phone calls, text messages, and emails begging me to come back. When those tactics didn't work he did a 180. He tried to get me in legal trouble by reporting false information to the police. I've never had a record. I don't have a history of violence. Suddenly the cops are calling and visiting me on a regular basis. My email, phone, and Facebook accounts had been hacked. My friends also felt the wrath by being impersonated and cyber bullied, bribed, and harassed by this man. He went as far as to stalk me by using a tracking device. With that piece of technology he was able to be everywhere I was and he used that to his advantage by disabling my car several times. I was still fearing for my life.

My son's life had been turned upside down, but I knew leaving was for the best because who knows how long it would've taken before my son also became the victim of this abuse. My teaching career was being threatened as well. I had to deal with a smear campaign on a public forum, not just by him but by people who had no idea of the facts about what I had been dealing with. I know I shouldn't care so much about what others think, but let's face it, that's how I ended up in this situation in the first place. I was trying to fix someone who was broken in hopes to fill the hole in my own soul.

I lifted him up as high as I could and everyone saw that. His family reappeared in his life and friends told him they were thankful he had found me. I became his martyr and that made me feel good.

Inevitably he came crashing down again and he was taking me with him this time. It's not a pleasure to take a day off from teaching to fill out paperwork for a PFA. I never wanted to do that because I didn't want to admit that his ex-wife was right about him.

She was the evil one wasn't she? It's certainly not an easy task walking away from a house that you've worked your ass off to purchase, move into, and transform into your home. It's not a joy to be living out of bags and not being sure of where you're going to stay from night to night. Sure I was able to stay in the house for a while, but even with the locks changed and friends and family staying with me, I couldn't sleep soundly. If someone is capable of scratching himself to make it look like you attacked him and then call the cops to have you cited for it in front of his own son, what else is he capable of doing? I gracefully handed over the keys to our home, regardless of his decision to not help me pay for the mortgage. I made sure to leave behind all of his belongings as well as a few items my boy could do without. Through all of this I remained relatively calm.

What kind of a man takes advantage of services for abused women, making a complete mockery of a safe place in which these people can turn? Even after being reluctantly served a PFA full of complete lies, I still somehow felt sorry for HIM!

Being sure to collect evidence and document everything along the way I was helped greatly by several police departments. The YWCA had some of the most caring people I had ever met and they became an invaluable source for me as I went through this nightmare. They helped me realize more than anything that I was doing the right thing and that I couldn't back down no matter what. My friends and family, who know me well, didn't need me to tell them much. They watched the craziness unfold before their very eyes. They didn't want any parts of him and did not need to be convinced by me, as he did the convincing on his own. As far as those who I had lost along the way, they had just been simply waiting for me on the other side. I can't believe I am that woman who endured the black hole of an abusive relationship, but somehow I found my way out. I don't think I even fit the stereotype profile of a victim. I'm not living on the inside any longer, and although it will take a while for my confidence to rebuild and my heart to heal, I feel stronger. I won't be able to hear my son and stepson laughing and playing together any more. I've lost my house, my first real garden, and my credit is ruined.

I'm left with more credit card debt than before and my house will be foreclosing. My reputation may be tainted among some communities of people who choose to ignore true colors. But what I need to realize now is that the strength I've gained from being able to walk away from all of this is something that no one can ever take away from me. I made it. I'm with that light that I knew was at the end of the tunnel. I am free. I am a survivor.

by Sabrina Duke

Red Snow

my mother wore blood

like a new winter fashion

almost proudly, often enough

that we thought it was normal

as we grew up, my sister and I

never did learn how to see the calm

her, cold and repressed

by everyday oxygen

clotting to keep out the human nature

me, warm and flowing

dripping across the floor

staining everything I touch

both of us,

like the blood we saw

on our mother as little girls

by Missi McLaren Ritter

Shatter Proof

I list all that is broken, in a house with no glass.

Nothing fragile survives.

My plants reduced to grit, dirt and smashed terracotta.

Pictures in shreds, frames splintered.

Hope of anything new is a waste!

Replaced mirrors will only show me shiny and happy

briefly,

followed by the twisted face reflected

in pieces from the floor.

The romance of hope is over, rage runs this show and it
is a show-down.

When we fight over stupid things

I lose myself in hysteria.

My shrieks are wounded-animal, an exorcism.

I am possessed and convinced the only way to conquer
the ass- kicking

is to out-crazy his ass.

"You want some of me! Keep hitting me, kill me,

come-on fucking kill me"

My words squeeze out high and strangled,

his long fingers closing over my voice box.

My words rise higher, black dots in my eyes.

He must love me, if he needs so much to destroy me,

he can't walk away.

I will not be silent, will not be ignored.

Fear of being unloved and alone curdles inside me,

regurgitated in rage, thick and sweet.

We kick and we scream and I embrace the physical.

Pain is real to me like nothing else.

I understand it in its badness.

It's a high like crack- is a high.

I lose consciousness white lights flash.

Stars, birds and bells.

A rush like whippets or Wite-Out

huffed from a brown paper bag.

I need this drama to exist.

Maybe this is what I'm addicted to.

Not that I like it. I hate it. I hate me. I hate him.

But we keep coming back to this.

The jolt of his punch, his kick gives blankness,

white noise, relief from thought.

Like the pass out game, the high you get from

shoplifting or looking at porn at work,

Waves of hot and cold

tingle towards numb limbs, eyes bubbly.

the sting of it gives me strength.

Convulsing without use of arms.

He's holding them so I bite.

How hard do you really have to bite to draw blood,

rip flesh?

Hard! Harder than it feels I can but firmly clenched

I never find out.

Though I am a beast sinking into him,

his fist lays my jaw open every time.

Things smash, the toilet lays slain, water fills the room.

The phone pulverized under size twelve shoes.

Why did I bother to buy the good one?

I'll wonder as I piece together what is left

and broken as the phone,

I will borrow ten dollars to buy the cheapest one

downstairs at Walgreen's.

The new phone will sit on bare floor

next to my mattress.

No cradle to hold it, just a stupid button to push.

When the neighbor's call the police he is led out in cuffs.

Spitting as if disgusted to have wasted his time.

I am pulled from under the shelf

in the back of the closet.

Cop faces question and never understand.

They examine torn photos of me and can't see

the resemblance.

Left alone I sob loud, a whooped child's wail.

I feel as broken as my surroundings.

My stubs of acrylic nails ache.

Never again...I say

until next time...

when he will beg me to open the door,

and I will.

Sorrow Is My Only Weight Loss Plan

I'm swinging a hammer at his windshield

he's trying to run me over

I'm in my underwear in a blizzard

his car hits the light pole

tires spin out in the snow

I'm screaming at him to remember this

remember me

next time you cheat on your wife

not sure if I'm a victim or a victor

so sure I'm nothing

as quick to melt as flakes on bare skin

It's the last I see of him

a man I thought I loved

The lovely starving I did after

the liquid diet tears and beer

chewing on my organs

teeth first

a grinding ball

of hated flesh and lonely bones

no part of me could see

past him

with his skinny wife

on the phone

telling me she's his wife she'll forgive him

they have a child

I held her daughter once

pretending I'd give her a sibling

I will ever smell

the milk spill in his backseat from when she wrecked it,

the day he wasn't at the Hospital door to pick me up,

the crushing cold snow banks outside the heated

automatic door

no phone in my apartment

how I lost everything

and dreamt of redemption through love

love for someone too drunk to own it, or return it

who would forget me quickly

settle back in his dysfunction junction

I had no business losing my cute quiet boyfriend for this

turning him into a domestic violence case at nineteen

making him homeless cause he couldn't love me

or just say that he did

and I wanted proof

in all my black eyed head-banging

all my hammer slinging knife wielding

I was looking for proof

maybe that I was real not so fake and empty

not another snowflake melting in spring

I was twenty five but

not sure I'd been birthed

still unformed and fetal

trying to swim back upstream

God it's ugly out here looking for love

and so, so cold.

by Cassandra Dallett

It's All Your Fault

"It's all your fault!"

That's what they say.

Treating you like an intruder armed with an AK.

But I recall, you were

Thrown against the wall

And punished unfairly

Like the apostle Paul.

You couldn't speak a word, let alone write a letter

'Cause they'd call you the whore of Babylon,

Hungry for pleasure.

Maybe you were lost and

Looking for Treasure and he

Led you to his chest

Which held chains and fetters.

You never wanted maggots in your hawk's nest.

You wanted to see keenly behind the bottom of a

shot' glass

Which was soiled and dirty,

A garden in which he planted

A seed of seduction which bloomed into his antics.

So ignore all the people who call you a whore still

And victimize the villain who forced you 'gainst your

will.

Forgive that villain

Although he may not be sentenced

Because he incriminates himself

For the size of his appendage.

by Soala Idasetima

Move On

I am no longer a victim but a survivor

Fear is no longer my master,

I killed it with courage

And erased my past from my present

Because past has nothing to do with present

I silence my negative thoughts with positive words

Rebuild myself- image to brand new

Because 2pac told me

There's a brighter day for me

If I can make it through the night

So, I became a warrior

Used loneliness to see clearly

That life is for warriors

Because loneliness is a mirror

Like the mind of Thick code

So, I move on with life like time

And begin to love myself more

Bring voice to the voiceless

Heal my pain with happiness

And I survive, like Maya Angelou

Am here today without regretting the past

Because I was born to be great

To be strong

So, I will forget the past

And move on with present

by Ogunsina Temi-tope

The Cycle

Deep gasps, loud beats and occasional shifting of human bodies entangled together. As his hand moved stealthily towards her bosom, she shrieked in pain. In pain, as she was, stood up and started comforting herself. The next moment her concern for herself was rewarded with a slap on the face.

"You won't get today's payment"

"But Saabji, I have an injury over there "

"So What? Just get up from here"

A shabby old house with wine bottles stacked in a corner, male boxers resting over two utensils kept on the floor. Aakriti was trying to search for her pencil amongst these as she was startled by something that she was now used to.

"No money? You witch. You enjoyed the whole night with that millionaire."

"He was not satisfied."

She was pushed, the injury on her bosom deepened.

Aakriti threw away the pencil which she had finally found and rushed towards her bleeding mother to pick her up. But this time the deepened injury had penetrated all her gasping attempts to survive.

Deep gasps, loud beats and occasional shifting of human bodies entangled together. As his hand moved stealthily towards her bosom. Aakriti didn't shriek in pain. She collected the money and left.

By Ekta Rawat

A Temporary Bobby-Soxer

For six months after, I wore bobby socks and a long skirt and occasionally sneakers. Certainly not anything resembling high heels. For years after, I was unable to get into an elevator with a male stranger. Even now, when I do, I sometimes huddle in a corner or stand close to the door to be able to make a rapid escape. It's never far from my mind.

For years, too, I had the sense of trauma, shame, and guilt of many victims—especially sexual assault victims. Only recently, when I told my daughters about the incident some 50 years later did I realize the impact it still had on me.

Both girls were shocked, and retroactively protective. Both of them had reached their 20s and hadn't experienced a single incident of sexual harassment or abuse. Maybe things have improved. Maybe ...

Since that episode in the elevator of an office building in Manhattan I've been groped and date-raped. Made uncomfortable by a few professors, including one who was later convicted of sexual abuse in a foreign country. Certainly I've heard of far-worse incidents of rape than my own, sometimes by strangers and sometimes by friends or family members. Some had led to torture or murder. But I never forgot the experience of being followed and assaulted by a man at the tender age of 14.

It was a particularly vulnerable period, too. My mother was in the hospital, I believe with a hysterectomy at a time such surgeries kept women hospitalized for a week or more. I was left with my father and brother, and felt I couldn't tell them what had happened.

Eventually I ended up seeing a therapist. He assured me that it wouldn't have made any difference if I were wearing a nun's habit, if I was 4 or 84. That men don't assault or rape because women are "provocative" or even for sexual reasons. I absorbed the message, and yet... When I see a scantily clad woman, I sometimes feel like shouting: Don't you know what you're doing? It's mind versus emotions.

The incident occurred during the first time I had ever taken the train alone from Brooklyn (where we lived) to Manhattan. It was for a mission of "vanity." The contact lens doctors I had gone to in my home borough were unable to fit me comfortably with hard lenses, so he suggested I see a specialist in Manhattan. It was broad daylight, and the farthest thing from my mind was danger.

A man—can't recall what he looked like, except he was thin and relatively short and neither young nor old—started talking to me on the subway. The train was crowded. It wasn't 6 in the morning or 10 at night, so I didn't give it any thought. I simply didn't answer. After all, I was used to construction workers talking to me, and New York was not the "silent," unfriendly place people imagined it to be.

Nor did I feel particularly alarmed when he got off at the same stop as I did. After all, people got off at the same stop all the time in New York. Plus, at that time I was what I've never been since—an "innocent."
Then I exited the train, and he was still there. The station was Union Square, certainly a busy area. Why I didn't go into a department store or look for a police officer? I don't know. That's part of the residual guilt. Maybe I just couldn't believe anything was going to happen. In my world in Brooklyn we had Holocaust survivors, but not domestic violence or sexual abuse

ones. Supposedly. Maybe I didn't think he'd do anything more than say some more chosen words to me and continue on his way. Plus it was a bright sunny day-- perfect weather. The kind that never made you anticipate anything negative or threatening.

So I kept walking, toward the eye doctor's building. Thinking I had shaken the guy. I walked into the elevator, and pressed the button to the doctor's floor. All of a sudden there he was. I was too shocked to even try to get past him, out of the elevator. The doors closed, and he grabbed me. Started to kiss me. I started to shake. No one had kissed me up to that point, not like that. I didn't even know the term for French kissing. I was a young religious-school student who had maybe held a boy's hand.

I tried to wriggle out of his grasp, but there was nowhere to go. Still, I was relatively lucky. When the elevator door opened at the doctor's floor, he let go. Didn't try to follow me. Had he been determined to go further, even during that short time span in the elevator, I suppose he could have. Thank God for that. But he left his mark nonetheless.

Years later, when I had just moved into Manhattan, a man got into the elevator of my new building and took out a knife. He was a mugger, probably drawn by my expensive-looking coat and "lost" demeanor. Because of what had happened years before, I didn't really think about the rings he took from me, though they had sentimental value. Certainly not about the few dollars I had in my wallet. I was amazed he didn't take the coat but was determined to sell it nonetheless. The only predominant thought I had was, Please don't rape me.

But on that bright, sunny day in Manhattan the nightmare wasn't quite over when the elevator door opened and closed. I learned then that for some men, even presumably decent ones, being the victim of sexual assault makes you suspect—and invites them to try something n their own. When I walked into the eye doctor's office hysterical and told him what had happened, he didn't really say anything. Maybe it was my imagination, but I don't think so. As he looked into my eyes to see what the lens problem was, I felt that instead of placing his hand on my shoulder, it rested closer to my chest. I couldn't wait to get out of there. A lot more "paranoid" and less innocent than I had been before.

by Barbara Trainin Blank

The Clothes I Was Wearing

originally published by Connotation Press *in 2012.*

October 31, 1976

It was just after two in the morning when I finally stepped outside the bar and paused to light a cigarette. Exhausted, I leaned against the wall next to the heavy oak door and smoked, watching the people I'd served drinks to for the last eight hours stumble past. It was Halloween, and everyone walking by was in costume, none of them elaborate or very creative: a gorilla mask worn with a flannel shirt and torn Levis, a skeleton crudely painted onto a pair of black long johns. What a waste of a holiday, I thought.

I was just 19 years old, barely old enough to legally serve drinks in the state of Louisiana. Tonight had been raucous, chaotic, the crowd fueled by alcohol and the opportunity to escape their day-to-day-lives through anonymity. Last call, when it finally came, was a blessed relief.

The night air was stale. The stink of alcohol and cigarette smoke clung to my clothes, and I could still hear the faint sounds of Willie Nelson on the jukebox inside the bar. I knew that it would be hours before I could sleep.

I ground my cigarette out in the gravel and walked towards the highway, where I hoped to catch a ride. I was meeting some friends on the other side of the parish line. In Louisiana, each parish, or county, has different liquor laws, and although the bars here in town were closed now, the one where I was going would be open for several hours.

Everything was quiet as I walked past the small shops and restaurants that lined the downtown strip.

When I reached the highway I stood on the corner under the streetlight. It was a two-lane road, and at this time of night there wasn't much traffic. I watched the eyes of the drivers as they passed, hoping one of them would stop. In my hurry to leave work I'd forgotten my jacket and it was too late to go back for it now. A car filled with Halloween revelers passed and honked but didn't slow down. I blew on my hands to warm them and lit another cigarette. No one stopped, and as time went on fewer and fewer cars drove by. For a moment I wondered if I should give up and go home. But just then a car pulled up to the curb and the moment was gone.

There were two men inside the car. They weren't much older than I was. The rear end of the car was jacked up and the engine was loud. I yelled over the noise to tell them where I was going.

"Club 190." I said. "Can you take me there?"

The man in the passenger seat got out of the car and stood holding the door open so that I could get in. At that moment I made a choice. I climbed in and sat next to the driver, scooting over so there would be room for the three of us. The man outside got back in and closed the car door. It was dark and I didn't look closely at either of them.

"Thanks for picking me up." I said.

The inside of the car was warm, and I was glad to be out of the cold. It was about fifteen miles to the bar where my friends were, so I settled in and tried to get comfortable.

As soon as we left the city limits we were instantly in what still seemed to me to be the middle of nowhere, although we were less than a mile from the middle of town. Even after living here for months I still wasn't accustomed to the vast expanses of dark open space. I'd grown up in California, and was used to streetlights and people everywhere, at all times of the day and night: gas stations, fast-food restaurants, 24-hour markets. Here the towns were miles apart, with nothing in between but the occasional house, and seemingly endless miles of pine trees. In the light from the car's headlights, the trees passed by in a blur.

The town itself was a beautiful little college town in the southeastern part of the state, not far from New Orleans in one direction and Baton Rouge in the other. I had moved here to attend the local university, where both of my parents had graduated. The weather was horribly hot and humid during the summer months, but the rest of the year wasn't too bad. I had friends here and had settled into a nice life. Louisiana was so very different. The food, the architecture, the local dialect; everything here was exactly what California wasn't. And for a while at least, that was a good thing. There were a lot of bars in town, and a lot of churches. My parents were married in one of them, a white church surrounded by huge oak trees draped in Spanish moss that I walked past every day on my way to work.

The men in the car didn't seem to want to talk, which was fine with me; I'd listened to people talking and yelling for drinks all night. So I chattered on about nothing in particular, oblivious to the fact that these men were much too quiet. After awhile I got tired of talking to myself and just listened to the radio. "Monster Mash" was playing, a song I'd suffered through countless times tonight already, when suddenly the car slowed and the driver made a left turn off the highway. Surprised, I turned to look at him.

"This is the wrong way. You just need to keep going straight."

"We know a shortcut." he said.

I thought about that for a second. I knew the area well enough to know there was no shortcut; it was straight highway all the way. Then, we turned left again.

"What are you doing? I told you this was the wrong way."

This time he didn't reply. After a moment we turned left once more, into a clearing set back into the woods. Now, I was frightened. We sat with the engine idling. The clearing was small and surrounded by dense thickets of tall pines. It was completely hidden from the road, not the kind of place you would just stumble upon. These men had clearly been here before.

"What are we doing here?" I asked.

Neither of them answered. The driver turned off the engine, plunging us into darkness. The tip of his cigarette glowed in the dark as he smoked. I listened to the ticking of the engine as it cooled. I looked back and forth at them in the silence, but they wouldn't look back at me.

Though I couldn't see them clearly, I knew I'd never seen them before tonight. In small southern towns, bars are a way of life. I had never seen either of them in any of the ones I frequented. But there were bars in town I never entered, where the men seemed angry beneath the surface and viewed all strangers as enemies. Instinctively I knew that these men came from a place that I would never fit in, and would always have reason to fear. I was pinned between them. But that hardly mattered. There was nowhere to run even if I could, no one to hear my call for help. How easily I gambled with my life then.

"You can't do this," I said, not yet knowing what 'this' was. "I know a lot of people. I have friends who'll come after you."

How naïve I was to threaten them. I told them I was having my period, that I had a venereal disease, some kind of STD. Surely there was something I could say to convince them to let me go. When I realized that there wasn't I began to cry. One of them told me to shut up then, that my crying was making him angry.

I did then what I suppose most people do when faced with the prospect of a terrifying unknown. I begged for my life.

"Please let me go." I said. "I won't tell anyone. Please, just let me go."

They both sat very still, staring straight ahead. I couldn't imagine why none of this was having any effect on them. I waited on young men every night from behind the protection of the bar. I served them Dixie beer and shots of cheap bourbon, told them dirty jokes and pretended to be their friend, calling on the bouncers for help if I ever felt any danger. I was used to being the one in control. It was part of my job. I tried to hold on to that control that was slipping away so quickly, which had, in fact, been gone the moment I'd gotten into the car. There were no bouncers here to help me now.

It was much later that I realized I had only seen their faces in profile. For a long time afterwards I wondered if that was so it would be harder to identify them later, should it come to that, or if they were simply steeling themselves for what they were about to do.

I have no memory of what happened when I got out of the car. I'm thankful now that I don't. I imagine myself standing in the cold, taking off my clothes, shivering, amazed that just an hour before I had been pouring Jack Daniels into plastic cups.

They must have been sitting in the dark watching me. Did I try not to show them how frightened I was so that they wouldn't get angrier? Did I hold my head down as I took off my clothes, and fold each piece before I put it on the ground? Did I stand in that clearing, naked and cold, my arms wrapped around my chest, thinking the same thought over and over again? I want to go home. I want to go home. I want to go home.

I don't remember getting into the back seat. I remember only images from the inside of the car, none of them specific or fully formed, except for one. My head is resting against the rear passenger door and I am looking at myself from a distance. I am watching myself looking up, not at the roof of the car, but through it to the sky above, to where I must have instinctively been searching for some kind of solace.

At nineteen, I was very skinny, with long brown hair. I was stubborn and sarcastic, a façade I was sure would protect me from any problems that came my way, when I thought about it at all. I was wearing blue jeans and a worn-out pair of Keds that night, but it is the blouse I wore that I remember most. Cream colored, woven, like macramé, with a cotton string threaded through the holes in the weave that I tied beneath my breasts. It was something a young girl could get away with wearing. I threw it away a few days after that night because I couldn't imagine ever wearing it again, but for some reason I have always associated that blouse with what those men took from me. To me it represented the loss of whatever innocence I had left.

I was years away from understanding the concept of post-traumatic stress, but in the weeks and months following that night, even I somehow knew that the mind does what it can to protect itself. My memory lapse is clearly defined, and corresponds almost exactly with the time I spent naked, with the time I was being raped.

I don't remember putting my clothes on again, but I remember looking at my purse, still on the floor of the car where I'd left it. I still have my purse, I thought. Why would such a thing matter? Neither of them had spoken yet, and we sat in silence. I wanted a cigarette badly but was afraid to ask for one or to reach for my purse. Finally one of them spoke.

"You're not going to tell anyone about this, are you?"

For a moment I thought I might be losing my mind. I'd already told them I had friends who would come after them. Now they were asking me if I was going to tell anyone. Nothing was making any sense. I only knew that I wanted to be anywhere other than where I was, somewhere far away from these men, from this car.

"No," I finally whispered. "No, I won't tell anyone."

The driver started the car then, and backed the car out of the clearing. He drove a few hundred feet, and once again stopped the car. The man on the passenger side got out. I heard him walk to the back of the car and open the trunk. Why have we stopped? I thought. Are they going to kill me now? I knew they had guns, not because I'd actually seen one, but because I'd seen the gun culture so prevalent in the South. Every local male I knew had one. My boyfriends slept with them under their pillows. More than once I'd reached out in the middle of the night and felt cold steel, wondering, what on earth do they need protection from?

I thought about my family then, but desperately tried not to. What was happening to me was so outside the realm of what I'd ever thought possible that my mind refused to accept it. I believe now that if they had killed me, my sisters, and my mother and father, would have been there with me. But at the one time in my life I needed to most, I tried not to think of the people I loved, because if I did I knew I might start to scream.

I didn't know what the man behind the car was doing. There was absolutely no sound. The driver sat next to me, silently smoking. It was if they were waiting for something. Were they trying to work up the courage to kill me? Had they stopped the car for a lost pack of cigarettes, or for a jacket left in the trunk? I will never know the answer to these questions because, unbelievably, they let me go. The man outside the car eventually got back inside. The two men hadn't said a word to each other. We drove back to the highway, and the man driving pulled over and told me to get out.

"If you say anything about this, we'll come after you," he said.

How utterly surreal it was to hear him say that. Of course I was going to say something. I was going to tell everyone I knew if I got out of the situation alive, or so I thought then. As they drove away I watched the taillights until they disappeared. Neither one of these men had even once looked me in the face. I felt, for the first and only time in my life, what it means to actually feel less than human.

As they drove away I stood on the side of the road, shaking with fear. Finally I could cry.

I stood in the dark and cried for a long time, eventually starting to walk in the direction of the bar where, I hoped, my friends were. There was no shoulder on the side of the road to speak of, just a thin strip of gravel. The ditch next to the road was too wide for me to jump across and on the other side there were only acres and acres of pine trees.

There was barely enough moonlight to allow me to see. The only sounds were my footsteps on the gravel and the sound of my breathing. I didn't know if they would change their minds and come back for me, and if they did, what I would do. I could tell when a car was coming up behind me from a long distance away, the headlights reflected on the yellow mile markers by the side of the road. Each time a car passed I began to panic, somehow keeping my eyes straight ahead and focused on the road in front of me. There was nothing to do except keep walking. There was no place to stop, nowhere to ask for help. All there was, in front of me and behind me, was the dark. I want to go home.

Eventually I saw the lights of the bar in the distance. I don't know how many miles I had walked. It felt like I'd been walking for hours, and, once I saw the lights up ahead, it still seemed to take forever to get there. When I finally crossed the highway to the parking lot, I saw a few cars that I recognized. Thankfully, my friends were still there.

The door to the bar was locked, but through the window I could see a bartender inside cleaning up. He looked up when I knocked.

"Sorry, we're closed," he said, when he came over to open the door.

"I know. I'm just looking for someone."

The lights were turned all the way up, illuminating the remnants of a party similar to the one I'd worked a few hours before. Orange and black streamers were everywhere, hanging from the ceiling and trampled underfoot. Discarded party masks were everywhere, vampires, witches, ghosts. Carved pumpkins with leering faces and melted pools of white wax sat on the bar next to half empty glasses, plastic go-cups, and overflowing ashtrays. I picked my way through the mess towards the back room, where I found my friends still nursing their last drinks and watching the band pack up their equipment.

"Where've you been? We were starting to worry!" They were flushed and happy, drunk from a long night of partying. So instead of the truth, I told them I'd stayed after hours to play pool and had lost track of time. One of them handed me a drink they'd ordered for me at last call and I went to find the bathroom. I splashed water on my face and dragged a brush through my hair. I went into one of the stalls and locked the door. I sat for a long time, my hands shaking, holding my drink, the ice now melting in the glass.

At the time, I lived by myself in a small wooden house next to the railroad tracks. The trains that came by during the night carried mostly freight. The passenger trains passed through on the other side of town, on the tail end of the City of New Orleans line, the train my friends and

I took into the city every year to celebrate Mardi Gras. The house sat between two cross streets, forty feet from the tracks, at the exact spot where the train's engineer unleashed a whistle heard for miles. Whenever a train came through, the house shook madly, rattling everything in it.

For months afterwards, with only my anger to keep me company, I lay awake in this house by the tracks. I stared out my bedroom window, watching the trains as they passed, fantasizing how I would kill the two men who had raped me. I would burn their houses to the ground, or shoot them as they left for work in the morning. "Why me?" I would ask them before they died. "Why did you do this to me?"

I never went to the police. I was a young girl in a small town in Louisiana, and the men who raped me were locals. My father had been born and raised in another small town not far from here, and several generations of Louisianans were my own flesh and blood. But if you weren't raised in the South you were an outsider. I may have been stupid enough to get into a car with two strange men in the middle of the night, but I was smart enough to know that the police wouldn't arrest those men, not then, or ever.

A few days after the rape, my two sisters and I were sitting at a small table in one of the local bars. They also lived in town and we saw each other often. The bar was dark and quiet, a place people came to drink, not to socialize. We sipped our drinks and made small talk, but I knew they were wondering why I had asked them there in the middle of the day. I was nervous and scared, even with the two people I trusted more than anyone. I stared at the table, fidgeting, fingering my cocktail napkin.

"Something happened to me," I said. They both became very still, as if somehow they knew what I was going to say. It was the first time I had ever tried to say the words out loud and I was having trouble speaking.

"I was raped," I finally said. They froze, as they tried to process what I was telling them. Then they both began to cry. If I had known how much pain it would cause them I would never have told them.

One of them told me recently that hearing about my rape affected how she viewed men for years afterwards.

My other sister can barely discuss it still, even after thirty years. I can lock it away, but they are left only with their imaginations. I never told my parents. My father is gone now, and my mother still doesn't know. She would be devastated by the thought of one of her daughters going through such a thing and I will always protect her from that. But these were my sisters. As they held me and cried, I grabbed onto the lifeline they offered: the unspoken words that told me I was loved, and that none of this was my fault.

When I was a child, my father used to sit me on his shoulders, and from up there the world seemed a very safe place. And back then it was a safe place. My sisters and I were raised in a middle class family with two parents that loved us unconditionally, shielding us from the dangers of the outside world through a dependable routine of Tuesday night meatloaf, homework, and church on Sunday. And while I lived an idyllic childhood reserved only for the very lucky, at the same time it was also a childhood that could in no way prepare me for what happened that Halloween night in October 1976. At the same time, it was precisely the kind of childhood that would sustain me in the years that followed, providing a lifeline for me when I lost my way, giving me something to hold on to when I did not know where to turn.

In the first few months after the rape, my thoughts towards these two men remained unyielding. For me, there was no reason or compromise. They deserve to die, I thought. I will make them suffer. I never considered the consequences of killing two men, possibly because somehow I knew that this was some sort of defense mechanism, a survival tactic. Still, I reacted in the only way I knew how. I didn't seek any help from anyone, and didn't recognize that I needed it.

When I reached out, for sympathy or for some kind of human connection, people rarely reacted the way I thought they would. I don't know what I expected them to say, but I was usually angered or hurt by their reaction, or lack of one. Looking back, I know my friends would never have purposely hurt me. But I couldn't see that then. What seemed like indifference was probably a simple inability to react to an abstract concept. Nobody wants to talk about rape if it has never happened to them. Before long I stopped reaching out at all.

It has been many years since that night. I still don't know who those men were. I don't know why they let me go. I don't know if they raped other women, which I now think about often. All I know is that I survived. But I did not survive unscathed. I was angry for a very long time, a toxic anger that is not always outwardly visible. I turned to self-medication, to drugs and alcohol, to help me forget, which worked amazingly well for a long time until, not surprisingly, they became the problem rather than the solution.

As the years passed, my anger became less acute. My thoughts of revenge eventually disappeared. What stopped me from acting on these fantasies was the possibility that those men, as hard as it was for me to believe, might have wives, children. And I probably just got tired of thinking about death.

I know now that there are layers of memory, and that you can choose which ones to peel back and examine. When it comes to certain events in your life, you can live only on the surface, never looking at what lies underneath, and that is exactly what I did: I internalized, buried, and denied the existence of my rape for over thirty years.

In December of 2007, I left my hotel in New Orleans and began the 60-mile drive to the town where I had been raped. As I drove, I struggled with my thoughts. Why am I so afraid? There's nothing there that can hurt me now. I passed through the French Quarter, and the neighborhoods ravaged by Hurricane Katrina. I'd been away from this small town for thirty years, and now I was going back, to search for a place I had hoped to never see again.

Thirty feet below the interstate, cypress trees stretched to the horizon. Herons perched on pine trees kept watch over the wetlands below, and pirogues, the small, flat fishing boats scattered throughout the bayous, were steered by fishermen a world away from my car high above them. Louisiana possessed a strange beauty that, for me, was unlike any other place on earth. This was still a place I considered my second home.

Home. The word had never held any real significance for me until after the rape. For me it would never again simply refer to a place. The concept of home became a state of mind, a feeling of safety, of trust, the freedom to let my guard down without fear. It would be a very long time before I understood how difficult home is to find once you've lost it.

When I reached my exit, I turned off the interstate and drove through the small town I had once known so well. I passed the bank where I had opened my first checking account, the Laundromat where I spent every Sunday morning during college, with handfuls of quarters and ripped-up paperback novels. The bars on every corner didn't look like they had changed much, the buildings or, I imagined, many of the men who drank there. I passed the corner where I had stood hitchhiking so many years before.

I kept driving, on past the city limits. The town itself had looked much the same, but out here nothing looked familiar. There were subdivisions that hadn't been here before, new construction, unfamiliar landmarks.

After a few miles I saw a road up ahead that looked familiar. I slowed the car and turned left. Suddenly the air seemed heavier, and I had to fight the urge to flee. Thick stands of pine trees lined the road on both sides. There were houses here and there that I didn't remember from before. I tried to guess their age. Were they here thirty years ago? There had been no houses on the roads I remembered from all those years ago. As I drove I forced myself to look to the left, for the narrow road that would lead to the clearing in the woods.

Over and over again I turned off the main highway, down each road that seemed familiar, but eventually they all started to look the same. None of them matched my memory of that night. Eventually I realized that it didn't matter if I found the clearing, that maybe it was better if I didn't. I had been so sure that if I saw it again I would finally begin to heal. But healing, it seems, can't be orchestrated or planned.

If there is anything positive about surviving a sexual attack, aside from survival itself, it is the knowledge that the concept of choice is something never to be taken for granted. These men took away my freedom to choose, if only for one night. In hindsight, I know that they were just boys. But they were boys who committed a horrible crime. They drove me into the woods in the middle of the night, calmly listened to me as I begged for my life, raped me, then left me like garbage on the side of the road.

How do you forgive an unforgivable crime? I don't know. Maybe you can't. For me, the key to healing has been acceptance, acceptance that this did happen and there is nothing I can do to change it. With that acceptance also came the knowledge that my life is no longer defined by that one night. Forgiveness, so far at least, has not been a requirement for healing. And while I know that someday it's possible I will learn to forgive, for now I choose not to.

by Sandy Ebner

I Choose to Live

Shattered Glass, broken noses, split lips, torn garments, clumps of hair at my feet, splatters of blood on the wall. They all flash in my minds' eye and might have been part of my journey, but shall not define me or the path I shall take.

To the dark eyes void of a soul that blasted through entry ways and expected respect through intimidation and fear. The child that is now a man sits and wonders; "Was coiling on a cold bathroom floor while holding a bruised and battered woman a new form of hide and seek I should've been aware of?"

Now, I live independently and smile every day, and my mother, your former rag doll, has regained her beauty, stands strong and fearless. She is now happy and in love in the arms of a real man, so, Thank You!

To the tall and charming man who took hold of my body uninvited and expected an "I love you." Your victim that is now a survivor sits and wonders: "Was my bleeding and stinging cheek a new kiss I had yet to try? Was your hand over my mouth a secret we were sharing? Were my muffled pleads and stream of tears not heard or seen? Was you taking a knife to my clothes while I trembled in fear a new art form I had yet to experience?"

Now, I date, experience romance and fall in love. I am confident in what I want for my life and do not hesitate in requesting it, so "Thank You!"

Now, I forgive you! Shocking isn't it? I do not forgive you because of the "I'm sorry", that you might have offered... I forgive you because my spirit shines far beyond the reach of your hatred and fear. You were unsuccessful in your ultimate goal... I forgive you for your lessons gave me strength, and I offer you the best revenge because I forgive you... Here's the best gift, the one that will erase your grin... I choose to LIVE!!!!

by Javier Cotal

Blood

Blood stealthily passed down my neck to the bosom but I stood unperturbed. For the first time, I could hear each time when my heart made futile attempts to shudder my soul with each beat.

August 14, 1947; the day well engraved in my each and every wound.

As I took steps to pave my way amongst hundreds of torn sarees and naked and bleeding women; my eyes tried to hunt for my mother amongst the dead.

Quite innovative they were, my sister was raped with an iron rod and my daughter after she died. Such an audacity I had that my body survived.

With Allah and Ram being summoned every moment, the last few days seemed the most religious ones. Probably they were. Probably blood was god's desire. Probably.

As I spotted my mother's face peeping out of the piled up mothers of the motherland, I rushed towards her to pull her out. But all in vain, it was just the head. The body was nowhere.

Naked, I was. Were I the naked one?

by Ekta Rawat

Sacrifice

I caught you under the maple

swaying under the falling leaves

singing to the sky

it was a lovely dream

even with the taste of metal in my mouth

leave this house

drive until your hunger passes

and your bones are stiff

the bridge is in disrepair

my bridge

my womb

that reached beyond broken

beyond broken we once were

once

rebuild in secret

I will follow

I will find you

by your heartbeat.

by Kara Valore

The Serrated Knife, a Ballad

His words cut like a knife, a dull serrated knife.

Had hopes for the future of becoming his wife.
His love he had won now dead shot with a gun!
Oh Lord why? Oh why?

His words cut like a knife, a dull serrated knife
Hopes and dreams for our future, for the rest of my life.
My dear sweet loving man, I did all that I can
To cherish and love him, the very best for a man.

I ask why Lord, Oh why?
Oh, his words cut like a knife, a dull serrated knife.
He promised to love me for the rest of his life.
One day he said softly, "Oh please be my wife."
His actions and words, became opposite, absurd!

Gone to pick up my ring, an "I promise to love you ring!"
But he shed his skin twice, oh God what kind of life,
Would I have with a man that turns things in to a slam?
Like Jekyll and Hyde, I would hate that whole ride!

And I said "Why, Lord oh why?"
His words cut like a knife a dull serrated knife
My love dead from his sharp words, with a dull cutting
knife.
It hurt worse than a clean cut, with a clean surgeon's
knife.
Yet he operated and co-operated, such a beautiful soul.

In his love's secret garden, he dug his own holes!
He pulled out all the flowers, and left all of the weeds.
He forgot in a garden love needs next Season's Seeds!!!
His love just an illusion, a ball of confusion.
How can a beautiful soul go out digging those holes?
Was it fear that crept in there? Don't think he is aware
Of his anger and his stare......not even aware!

Oh why, Lord oh why? His words cut like a knife
He just lost his next wife. All my hopes and my dreams
Dashed from that whole numbing scene.
All 'cause he cut out my life, my loves gone with that strife.
My love died on that night, with his dull cutting knife.
I won't stand for abuse and there's never an excuse!
Love cut out by his knife, so I won't be his wife.

Oh Lord why, oh why?
My sweet loving man has now shed his first skin
Oh where's my old sweetheart, all this made my head spin?!
I had love for this man, don't know where to begin.
Let love walk in my door, he was an angel before!
'Till there came out a man, from a faraway land.

Oh Lord why, oh tell me why!
His words cut like a knife, a dull serrated knife.
I've picked up my pieces, and gone on with my life.
He seemed shocked when I left him, and went on with my life.
His words cut like a ....knife.

by Sandi Leonard Polvinale

Weight

previously published in my book "Silence, Inhabited" (NeoPoiesis Press)

i.

most of all

i remember being held down;

riding my bike

and then

on top of me

(never above me – not for a moment)

suffocating, excruciating weight

ghoulish, contorted masks -

many in succession;

(many more, once the word got out...)

i knew them, i am sure

knew each of them

sometimes i knew their names

sometimes their faces

but i did not know

not then

not now

(never knew - not for a moment)

their reasons

for feeding on pain

pain for themselves

pain for others

as a wide-eyed nine-year old

in the canned goods aisle of the local IGA

a musky presence fumbled from behind

as i was carried

through flapping, filmy, filthy thermal fridge

to a back alley

minutes-like-hours later,

a grimy quarter was pressed into my hand

with a slumbering admonition –

be a good boy and don't tell.

i did not tell;

could not have told –

i only told my mother i had found a quarter

'a whole quarter?'

'i'm not sure, mother...

it has no face.'

ii.

many missing faces and

two decades later

i learned to disappear

although i could no longer feel the weight,

in quiet moments

i pondered whether or not

Bernouli's principle

applied to the human form

dreaming all the while

of tall buildings

and release

i did not understand

(never understood - not for a moment)

how i could invite the faceless ones

when others like them had caused so much pain

how i could keep inviting them

again and again

here

now

so long after

the weight had gone

as a child

i could not resist;

no longer a child,

i could not desist -

disappearing had become so easy

i did not see
(never saw - not for a moment)

that i had a choice...

they followed me,

the faceless ones, and

i followed them —

i disappeared nightly;

they never did

iii.

once

in the twilight

between decades

(just once)

i took a deep breath

and, hovering in the limbo between

helplessness and invisibility,

watched myself say

no

watched as

the monosyllabic archangel of my nascent redemption

escaped my blown lips

only to be snuffed out

by the weight of a grimy hand

try as i might

i could no longer disappear

i stayed, then

raping myself anew in my silence

i did not cry
(never cried – not for a moment)

Bernouli was a charlatan

iv.

one stifled summer Sunday

i flipped that faceless quarter;

that badge of crippling cowardice,

now a talisman of misbegotten Providence –

flipped once

(tails!)
and began a crime spree

shoplifting only what i did not need;

sneaking it all back later

distracting turgid, thick-waisted security guards

with anonymous. androgynous whispered solicitations

in my fantasies

they ran me down

they punished me

i did not consider
(never considered – not for a moment)

the possibility of a life without fear

this ended

as unexpectedly as it had begun

on the winged, leaden morning

when first i considered the possibility

of an identity

without fear

v.

now

middle-aged

stout

happily married

i am

a teacher –

respected, revered

living abundant dreams (nightmares' progeny)

having long since forgiven my silent former self –

as it turns out

i did not believe

not then

not now
(never believed – not for a moment)

that the faceless ones

were inside me to stay

now that they no longer appear

now that i no longer disappear

now that i

my own archangel

have ascended...

i,

reborn,

ponder Bernouli

and struggle

with

weight

by Rich Follett

Sex Ed In These United States of Amurika:

It's up to the parents

Do NOT have sex.

Save it for marriage.

Sex is dirty and can give you a disease

that's really all you need to know, now put on that

purity dress, and go to the ball with your father

and then there's the sex ed that starts in late

elementary school.

Sought out by every young fella on the interwebs

teaching them how to treat a girl and really enjoy it

not as a mutual act of consent

but by slamming her in the eye with a money shot

and learning to see a her as less than human:

a dick sheath

a come dumpster

a set of holes existing only to see how many men

can fit inside of her

as she passively tolerates gagging

to the point of vomiting

or at the very least, to the point of tears

and obediently bends over to be torn.

And sometimes existing, lest we forget

as a target for male excrement

this coercion to this rape culture

has lulled us to sleep

and we keep our eyes happily closed.

And just keep tapping our feet

to song after song

from what's in this drink?

Baby its cold outside

to Thick telling you

you know you want it

to Pharrell saying he's

gonna give you something big enough

to tear that ass in two

as rapper after rapper

spews the stench of hyper-masculinity

through rape threat after rape threat

in song after song:

night time is the right time for creepin

vandalize your crib, rape your wife while she's sleepin

I'm all up on your bitch means I'mma rape her

all I got for these hoes is dick, duct tape and a stapler.

We could go on forever

but let's use this time together

to see and hear this epidemic of male sexual entitlement

and the fact that we keep grinding and twerkng along

to its theme songs

you see, playing along with this dominant arrogance

or even remaining silent in the face of it

makes us complicit

because until we speak up to build a consent community

we'll never get to a place of respect for our shared

humanity

and until enough men who have the strength to care

can represent that that there's no sexy in sexism there's

only a deepening schism within surrounded by silence

that perpetuates

this culture of violence.

Because until you see her, lying there staring at the

ceiling

or notice the tears running down her cheek

and until you hear the silence and the lack of a clear,

sober, enthusiastic

YES,

you are lacking consent.

And until you respond to

"oh yeah, dude

I'd do her"

Do you hear that?

"Do" her

To act upon...

You've missed your cue

to speak up in protest

because you cannot awaken respect for our shared

humanity

by muttering under your breath helplessly

you see its simple, really...

we got to get so loud that the ground shakes

to help us awake from this lullaby

that keeps us in bed with

this culture of rape

by Adele Ulrich

The Story of a Woman

This is the story of the 600 block of West Market Street

This is the story of the lady in apartment 2b

who screamed NO to the wall before choking

on a mouthful of sheet

there is no pillow that feels soft

when pressed against the back of your neck

This is the story of a woman who never suspected

because domestic violence doesn't happen if you have an

education,

if you have a decent job,

if your bruises can stay hidden beneath facades of

makeup

and a clip on ponytail

Besides, men don't abuse when they pay union dues

at a good job and go to church on Sunday...right?

This is the story of a woman who learned that a man

will beat you anyway

if he wants to, and the drink and the devil get in him

This is the story of a woman who had nowhere to go

and was told that shelters were dirty and worse than

the prison

she was already in - plus you can pick your poison but

I'll take your kids

and turn them against you

This is the story of a woman who finally said FORGET

YOU

This is the story of a shelter resident turned shelter

volunteer

This is the story of "He hit me last week" becoming

"I haven't spoken to him in two years

and I can finally sleep through the night"

This is the story of a woman who finally stopped

fighting

and let someone who cherished her inner beauty love

her

This is the story of a woman who loved herself a little

more each day

Who can share with others a story that involved

violence, even rape,

but that doesn't involve shame,

not anymore.

This is a story of a woman with a pen

who can release her beginning

because she writes her own ending

by Carla Christopher-Waid

Injuries 1990

I heard the change in Anthony's voice. He was in the driver's seat with his head down. He wasn't looking at me, but suddenly I heard the growl of a stranger. "Fuckin' Bitch"

My hand instinctively shot for the door handle. I got the door open. He was turning towards me in the passenger's seat preparing to hit me "You Bitch" the voice of a stone cold woman beater.

I was running as soon as my feet hit the ground. My legs stiff, my shoes slippery on the damp grass. He was right behind me. It seemed I was flying across the grass, but not fast enough I felt him grab my hair I was jerked and fell flat on my back. He started stomping on me. I tried to cover my face. I could feel my acrylic nails snapping off. It felt like my fingers were breaking. His foot was coming down again and again; I felt my head would flatten like a cartoon. I struggled onto my side; feet raining down on my shoulders, arms, back. Somehow I got to my feet and started running again. He was behind me, cussing me out the whole time. My brain was too panicked to comprehend his words, eyes wet in the rushing cold air, one ear already dead. I ran the rest of the way across the green, hit the sidewalk and straight across the four lanes of deserted street.

There was nobody, not one person in any direction. I made it to the other side of the street. I was screaming now, yelling "Help me, he's going to kill me" I ran past all the mansions along Marina Green, not so much as one light on. I swerved running back into the street across, and back through the grass. I didn't want to fight. I had never run from a man in my life, I fought. I was usually fearless. But this time, I wasn't mad, I wasn't passionate. I hadn't done anything wrong, for once in my life I hadn't done anything wrong.

Moments before we had been talking laughing, him trying to convince me Big Daddy Kane had AIDS that it had been on Oprah. He was really crazy. He just made shit up. I was dealing with a mad man you can't fight a mad man, you get away, you survive.

Still I ran, him breathing down my neck. I reached the ocean, could run no further. I climbed over the edge. Down the concrete wall into the water. I would rather drown. I didn't care. Before my feet touched rock or water, he was over me, grabbing my arm and dragging me up the cement wall. I felt my blouse ripping open the buttons flying off, my skin scraping concrete. My shoe fell into the water. He pulled me up onto the ground.

We were bathed in blue light, Police lights. Finally they were here. The policemen led me to a curb. I sank to the ground sobbing and hyperventilating, holding my shredded shirt together. I couldn't talk, couldn't move. I was shaking.

They leaned him face forward on the squad car and handcuffed him. They were running his name on the radio. I knew he had warrants so they would take him. He started talking to me over his shoulder, crying "Baby I love you. I'm sorry," It went on and on.

Could he possibly be saying he loved me, right now? I just sat there sobbing.

The cop standing over me got pissed, telling me, "Don't listen to him, you can do so much better. You're a beautiful girl."

How did he know I was a beautiful girl? I was a monster. My face had NIKE imprinted on it. My fingers looked like bruised sausages. "You have to leave him. How well do you know him? Is he your boyfriend?"
I just nodded and cried. I couldn't respond. An ambulance arrived, they led me to it and I climbed in,

lay on the gurney. It was my first time riding in an ambulance.

They took me to the police station on Fillmore Street. I had never been inside this station before it was still pretty new the first thing they built before the high rises full of white people moved in.

They asked me questions and took Polaroid pictures of my face. I was drunk and wounded, a beat up animal caught in the spotlight. When I saw the pictures I looked deformed a crazy, elephant lady. I wondered what the cop's thought of me, was it disdain for another white girl fucking with a black guy or did they actually feel sorry for me. I worried people would say I told you so. I felt like a fool my shame as painful as his betrayal.

They put me back in the ambulance and took me to General Hospital. They rolled me in and left me laying there on the gurney. My ears were ringing I couldn't hear out of the right ear. They left me waiting in a cold hallway. It was late, early morning hours there was a clock above the double doors. There was no one around. I had no one to call. I was alone in the world. I waited for what seemed like hours. I was so cold. I wanted my bed.

What were they going to do when they did take me through the doors? Really, what could they do for me? My pain couldn't be bandaged. I climbed down off the gurney awkwardly and limped out of the emergency room into the dark. I was barefoot my stockings ripped, biker shorts, and two little pieces of material that used to be my shirt.

There was no bus in sight. I had no money. I started walking. General Hospital was a long way from Haight Street, two bus' rides normally. I limped down Potrero Street. My head buzzing with thoughts about my life. How I appeared right now like a broke down prostitute, how really I was broke on the inside, shattered into pieces that I couldn't make sense of. I didn't want anyone to see me like this.

A small truck stopped, the driver an older black man wearing a Muni Bus driver's uniform, coming from or going to work. I didn't hesitate to get in his truck. I knew all the reasons you're never supposed to get into cars with strangers, but what could he do to me that wasn't already done? He could rape and murder me if he wanted to at least it would put me out of my misery.

It was warm in his truck, there was music playing softly. He asked me where I lived, said he'd take me. I told him yes it was my boyfriend that had done this. He told me without judgment I didn't need that shit. He took me home. I thanked him.

I climbed up the stairs and into my bed. Every part of me hurt, my head, face, hands, arms, my body, but none so much as my broken heart and confused brain. I could hear the things he'd said to me, the names he'd called me. I could not stop hearing his crying and pleading. When he'd said, "I love you" Some small part of me opened up just for a minute like "you do?" Like "doesn't love make everything all right? Couldn't that make it all better?" and then I felt so mad and ashamed of myself for feeling that way.

The phone rang. He was using his one call to call me, to tell me he loved me. He was sorry blah, blah, blah. I didn't hang up right away I just held the phone. I deserved to hear someone loved me, even if it was a lie. Even if he didn't know what love was, had never felt an ounce of it.

After listening to Anthony's shit for a few more minutes, I got my own shit together enough to respond. I described to him the injuries he had inflicted on me to give him something to think about. I told him I was never going to speak to him again, that he could stay in jail and when he got out not to contact me.

I called my boss. The last thing I wanted to do was go back there, to that smoky room full of prying eyes, women ready to tell me what I should have done what I shouldn't have done. Back to ringing phones of desperate, horny and lonely men with their dicks in hand. They were looking for something I didn't have to give, couldn't even pretend to.

I stayed in bed for a couple of days, as long as I could. I tried to avoid my roommates in the hallway. I took a cab downtown and bought a little TV for my room so I wouldn't have to come out. I wore big shades but they couldn't hide the bruises. I could have told strangers I had been in a car accident if my head wasn't still ringing with the sound of foot on flesh, Fucking Bitch and I love you, looping over and over in my head. The words no one wants to hear and the words everyone wants to hear all mixed up in a bitter pill. I couldn't take a breath without flashing on the night's events, without thinking of all the times we'd laughed in his car, the way he would sing along to every song on the radio but change the words so "Something In My Heart" was "Something In My Yard" and the whole song would be a garden theme, and how we always sang along to "Let's Chill" by Guy.

No one was going to get his crazy look before sex and say, "I've gotta get this nut
off my chest" One day we had sex in a hurry, he was late for a court date so he didn't shower. He had pulled out and cum shot way up on to his chest. He wiped it off but didn't shower. In the courtroom he turned to me and said "I gotta get this nut off my chest" sending me into hysterics, the judge glaring at us. This was the stuff I would miss, it was stupid, but I was lonely.

I had bills to pay. I had to keep a roof over my head, so eventually I went back to work. That first shift I lingered outside on the corner of 24th. Finally I sucked it up and went in. I had to take my shades off inside the dark office revealing the bruises. I told Mary Saint Mary, the manager, what happened and as people came in, I told my story in as little detail as possible. I didn't want to tell them at all but they could see my face, there was no way to pretend he hadn't beaten the shit out of me.

Everyone knew what had happened and who had done it. I felt like crying every minute of that first night. They wanted to know if I was still with him, wanted to convince me he had been cheating on me, like that would make it easier to leave him. Hearing it only hurt me more.

My co-workers said that Chickie, a girl we worked with, had told them that one night after Anthony and I had dropped her off, that he had gone all the way back to Oakland, banging on her door and calling her name. I called her a liar. But I wasn't sure. I was drunk that night and had gotten into an altercation with my upstairs neighbor before Anthony got back from parking the car. Maybe it had been long enough for him to go back to her house. That same night I had caught him holding Chickie's hand just for a second. I had asked what they hell was going on and they had both accused the other of grabbing their hand in a drunken moment. I had been pissed and eager to drop her off. She didn't like the guy we had brought along for her.

The phones were ringing. I hated the phones. I didn't want to talk to men, any men.
Men will lie to you, fuck you, and kick you when you're down. If you fuck them you are always a slut, if you don't you are a bitch.

I went through the motions at work. The goal is to keep the masturbating man on the other end of the phone talking for twenty minutes, and then you hang up on them, after convincing them to call you back. My voice was not sexy or upbeat. I wanted to tell them to go fuck themselves but they already were.

I tried to block the swirl of thoughts about Anthony cheating on me. My stomach was a gurgling mass, cramping and dropping out from under me, a rollercoaster of nerves. I felt like I was going to have diarrhea. I couldn't eat, had barely slept. I made it through my shift, clocked out and went home.

Two days later in my loneliness, I called an ex-boyfriend. I thought, even though he had beaten me up too, he really loved me. We had been together almost two years. He had lied. He had messed me up but even now he would want to see me. The sex would be good.

He came over. I let him see my face. He didn't feel bad or sorry for me. He said, "Damn, you got fucked up!" I smiled mortified, more embarrassed than I thought possible. I told him who did it. I tried to keep it light, like I wasn't heartbroken, like it was nothing. This was a touchy scene because you never want your ex to think of you with someone else, especially someone from the neighborhood. He already knew too many of my secrets and now I had let him see me weak and defeated.

He laughed at me, told me everyone knew Anthony was a woman beater from way
back, from High School, Junior High even. "Well I didn't know," I said "No one told me." He just shook his head. Told me to turn off the lights.

We had sex.

Then he left.

He called me early in the morning I was still asleep. He said he needed to pay the studio rent. He was a rapper now. Something about a check and could I give him a hundred dollars, he would give me a check his Mom gave him. I said "Yeah" sleepily. He came right by. We exchanged a check for cash.

Later in the day, I picked up the check to go cash it and realized it was useless. It was his mother's check but it was written out to him and signed by him. I couldn't cash this and he knew it. I called him demanding my money. He laughed at me and said I wasn't getting it, as calmly as if he was giving me directions, just matter of fact.

I was hysterical, threatening him, and demanding my money. I told him I was coming down to his Mom's house to break out all her windows. I was going crazy throwing chairs and swearing.

I threw down the phone. I had been beaten up, fucked over, and ripped off. That night as my roommates looked on I cut off half my hair.

The next day I bought a gun.

by Cassandra Dallett

~~Betraying~~
Reclaiming Sovereignty

Every woman, lady and girl is a goddess.

A woman of intuitive healing power.

Glowing light flows from her soul like the illuminating

star blazing in a day.

A heat of gold loving the serenity of pure essential peace

within.

Her body a temple of honor.

Not something to be possessed and dishonored.

Hearts entwined; lustful eye.

I'm Not your property,

Though you claim I am.

Your body screams with rage.

Blame.

Her body a temple of honor,

Your heart dishonors,

Making her,

Making me,

Feel that My body is your possession,

Your obligation,

To fulfill Your needs as a man.

What happened to a relationship of equality?

Your mind runs in a world of Patriarchy.

All she wanted was Sovereignty over her own body!

And you made her feel unwholesome, weak and less of a

woman for not satisfying your sexual desires as a man.

You took your claim, your prize as the silent tears fell

from her eyes.

Her heart breaking, tired of endless fighting, giving in...

It will be over soon.

You release your sin leaving her heart worn and thin.

In your eyes it was my obligation,

Your right as a man.

My body IS a temple of honor,

Your heart, Your mind, Your soul dishonors.

Yet, you still don't see...

The betrayal you caused

For taking away her Sovereignty.

by Aylish Steed

Hurricanes

Women

are coming in the form

of hurricanes

to teach men a lesson

no more corruption

no more corporate greed

no more cuts in social programs

no more trampling on human rights

no more destruction to the environment

no more war

The power of the matriarchy

will wipe out the male ego

and replace it with a

kinder, gentler society

Women

are coming in the form

of hurricanes
to teach men a lesson

and the waves

are going to come down

like machetes

to cut off every tongue

of every man who cursed them

to cut off every fist

of every man who abused them

to cut out every throat

of every man who murdered them

and cut off every dick

of every man who raped them

Katrina and Rita and Wilma

is just the beginning

we'll be calling the big ones

hurricanes Nzinga

and Nefertiti and Makeda

we'll be calling the big ones

hurricanes Harriet and

Sojourner and Ida B.

we'll be calling the big ones

Rosa and Coretta and Fanny Lou

Women

are coming in the form

of hurricanes

to teach men a lesson

never again will women be

blamed for falling out

of God's favor

never again will a bible

justify man's absolute reign

over the planet

never again will books

written by male jealousy

and fear oppress and subjugate

women

and never will there be

another story about

a woman being made from

a dumb trifling pitiful

caveman's rib

There will be no more priests

banging boys

no more pastors

banging housewives

and no more

Jimmy Swaggarts crying

crocodile tears on TV

after banging

sex workers in motels

The patriarchal clergy

will be wiped out and replaced

by authentic healers

and medicine people

and the planet will be restored

to its natural order

Women are coming in the form

of hurricanes

to teach men a lesson

no more baby daddy drama

no more chasing child support

no more down low scheming

no more lie detector tests

and no more private investigators

They are going to smack these

men to the ground

and make them get on their

knees and pray

as they shout to them

who's wearing the belt buckle?

who's wearing the pants?

who's your daddy now, bitch?!

Then all men

will be like the examples

that some men

have already set for them

They will be

accountable for their actions

attentive to their duties

and available for their families

Women

are coming in the form

of hurricanes

to teach men a lesson

because they are sick and tired

of being sick and tired

and men still consider them

a joke

until which time they'll discover

the joke is on them

hell hath no fury

like a woman scorned

There will be

no more suicides

no more genital mutilations

no more eating disorders

no more preventable diseases

no more unnatural deaths

And when it is all said and done

and order is completely restored

women will no longer have

to come in the form of hurricanes

they can just be

water.

by Ron Williams

A Look Inside the Mind of an Abuse Victim (Letter)

The recent media attention concerning Baltimore Raven Ray Rice and his brutal assault on his fiancée has prompted an increased interest in domestic violence. Typically individuals make judgments, ask questions and are intrigued to understand why and how can this happen.

The terrible truth is that domestic violence happens every day and is more prevalent than many major illnesses combined. What makes domestic violence particularly insidious is that it most often occurs behind closed doors. It is hidden from the public and its consequences are too many to name but extend into a lifetime and community for years to come. Violence is contagious and family violence is at the core of most street violence, crime, substance abuse etc.

Domestic violence is not a single assault but rather a pattern of abuse involving the exercise of power and control. Most of the victims we serve have experienced emotional abuse, denigration and captivity.

(Below is a representative account of the experience of a domestic violence victim. It should be understood that each domestic violence victim's experience is unique and cannot be easily encapsulated in a single account.)

Living in a cage waiting for the strike
I am living in a cage waiting for the strike. I am your sister, daughter and your best friend. I am you.
I am a battered woman. The cage is my life held captive in an abusive relationship. From the outside you can't

see the bars or feel the persistent terror that surrounds my every minute.

I can be found in every corner of your community, and I am the rich and the poor alike, the old and the young. I come in all colors and dream the same dreams you dream.

Every nine seconds I am beaten by a man and three of me are killed by a man each day. I wear my pain like an ugly dress but you will not see it. I am a social actor. If you ask me how are things? With heavy breath, full of shame and dishonesty, I will state everything is good. I will give you a thousand yard stare as I shrink back into my cage. We don't speak of family matters. What happens inside a family is private, they say. A private hell. I live with the ghost of what could have been.
My washcloth is just like yours, and it wipes away the forbidden tears and the blood of a violent marriage time and time again. I don't remember the safety of once upon a time.

I am stranded in the now with a man who, as a boiling pot, erupts and recedes with the venom of a brutal tongue and a clenched fist. Up and down the cycle goes all the while waiting for the inevitable strike. I am worthless and his words tear my entire being apart.

I love him, I think. I feel the strange need to protect and understand him. I explain his behavior away. Maybe I can find the one thing to change him or by believing him when he apologizes and starts the cycle again.
It's not his nine-pound hammer I fear or the way his bloodshot eyes chase me. It is my broken body and broken spirit cornered in a world without hope that leaves me empty.

One day he will kill me and leave my children as orphans to a world of violence. This I know.
I pray but no god answers. I scream but have no sound. I cry but my tears are dry.

I have learned to hate all men. I know full well that there are well-meaning men, but why don't they take action? How come men don't speak out? How come they allow this to continue?

Why do I stay? You don't know the many barriers I face to leaving. Money, a home, a job, fear, love, my children and my self-worth all are obstructions.

I don't want you to see me or see right through me. But I and my sisters need to be seen.
I have been away from me for so long.
I am living in a cage waiting for the strike. I am your sister, daughter, and your best friend. I am you.

by Rick Azzaro, Chief Services Officer of YWCA York

Support ACCESS York- YWCA York. Help us to help those who need us.

You have heard our voices, now we need
you;
Please do not remain silent
Speak out and Act loudly
Join us as we work to eliminate violence
toward women
Please show your support to those in need.
For more information go
to: www.ywcayork.org
If you, or someone you know, need our help
or just wants to talk, please reach out.

Domestic Violence: 1-800-262-8444

Sexual Violence: 1-800-422-3204

Thank you.
ACCESS York/ Victim Assistance Center/
programs of the YWCA York

Daniel de Cullá is a Poet & Writer. Painter & Photographer. Member of the Spanish Writers Association. Founder and Editor of the reviews of BodyArt, Art and Culture GALLO TRICOLOR, and ROBESPIERRE. He participates in Cultural Acts of Theatre and Performance. Ambassador of the Word by Museum of the Word. He's living between Burgos, Madrid and North Hollywood.

Carla Christopher-Waid fourth Poet Laureate Of York, PA was born in rural Virginia and brings the gypsy voices of her upbringing in the mountainous missionary compounds of North Carolina, the creature riddled forests of Michigan, the haunted subway tunnels of New York City, and the chaotic circles of Washington D.C. to her poetry. She is currently the host of Culture & Main; York's Weekly Cultural Showcase on WRCT, co-director of Community Arts, Ink / PoemSugar Press; York's Independent Press and an instructor with the Performing Arts Program with The Strand-Capitol Performing Arts Center

Javier Alberto Cotal is the oldest of three children. He was born prematurely with cerebral palsy in Ponce, Puerto Rico and was raised there until the age of 10. Javier has been writing poetry since the age of 13 and has published a few pieces on Poetry.com. He has lived in New Jersey, Florida and New York. He has currently been a resident of York, Pennsylvania for 14 years now.

Cassandra Dallett lives in Oakland, CA. Cassandra is a Pushcart nominee and reads around the San Francisco Bay Area often. In addition to several chapbooks, she has published online and in many print magazines such as Slip Stream, Sparkle and Blink, The Bicycle Review, Chiron Review, River Babble, and Up The River. A full-length book of poetry, *Wet Reckless* was released from Manic D Press May of 2014.

Sabrina Duke is a fourth-grade teacher, singer-songwriter and mother of a 9-year-old boy. After my divorce to my son's father, she got involved in a three-year abusive relationship with a man who also had a son. She left in 2012 and wrote this piece shortly after. The YWCA/ACCESS York helped her a great deal when she left the relationship, and she continues to volunteer and be an advocate for this program

Sandy Ebner lives and writes in Northern California. Her essays have been published or are forthcoming in the *San Francisco Chronicle, Connotation Press: An Online Artifact, Dead Mule School of Southern Literature, The Doctor T.J. Eckleburg Review, Bent Country*, the *HerStories/ My Other Ex* anthology, and other publications. She writes about a variety of topics, but is most interested in social and cultural differences and how they influence our lives. Her essay, 'The Clothes I Was Wearing' was named a finalist in both the 2012 Press 53 Open Awards and the 2012 Glass Woman Prize, in addition to being nominated by Connotation Press for a Pushcart Prize. She holds a Bachelor's Degree in Journalism from California State University, and is an alumna of the Community of Writers at Squaw Valley. She currently serves as Creative Nonfiction Editor at *MadHat Lit* and *MadHat Annual*.

Rich Follett is a High School English, Theatre, and Mythology teacher who has been writing poems and songs for more than 35 years. His poems have been featured in numerous online and print journals, including BlazeVox, The Montucky Review, Paraphilia, Leaf Garden Press and CounterExample Poetics, for which he is a featured artist. Three volumes of poetry, *Responsorials* (with Constance Stadler), *Silence, Inhabited,* and *Human & c.* are available through NeoPoiesis Press (www.neopoiesispress.com). He lives with his wife Mary Ruth Alred Follett in the Shenandoah Valley of Virginia, where he also pursues his interests as a professional actor, singer/songwriter, playwright and director.

Jennifer C. Foxworthy was born and raised in York, Pennsylvania. Once she graduated high school from William Penn Senior High in 1991, she embarked on a journey that would lead her into an illustrious career serving in the United States Navy. Jennifer served her country proudly for 21 years (September 23, 1991 to April 30, 2013) retiring as a Chief Petty Officer (E-7). Excerpts from my book "Tomorrow My Sunshine Will Come: Memoirs of Women Who Survived Domestic Violence" written by Jennifer C. Foxworthy and self-published through CreateSpace.com

Wayne Hislop is a chef from Ireland who in his spare time writes poetry.

Ron Kipling Williams is the star of the one man show, 'Dreadlocks, Rock 'n Roll & Human Rights' He is a performance poet and community activist residing in Baltimore, Maryland.

Pam McMillin has been writing poetry for six years. She lives in Mechanicsburg and frequently travels to York and Harrisburg to share her work at open mics. 'Your Pain, My Heart' is the story of the heart shaped tattoo on her back. She got it after recovering from a difficult relationship with a pill addict. Since then Pam has been busy in the dating world looking for Mr. Right. She had an experience with non-consensual sex, and prays for the day "Yes Means Yes" laws come to PA.

Christine O'Leary-Rockey is a poet, scholar, and former professor of Humanities living outside of Harrisburg, PA. She is a charter member of The (almost) Uptown Poetry Cartel, and her writing has been published a variety of venues, including Harrisburg Magazine, Shirazad, Planet Magazine, The Experimental Forest, Steel Pointe Quarterly, Megaera Magazine, Central PA Magazine and The Tarnhelm. She holds advanced degrees in Religion and Interdisciplinary Studies and is still combing the want ads weekly for that ad that reads, "Philosopher wanted for our busy office...will pay well." She is the author of "A Human Auction." and co-author of CowParade: Harrisburg, Pennsylvania. She was nominated for a Pushcart Prize in 2007. She is currently working on her next collection, 'The Gospel of Junkie Tom'.

Sandi Leonard Polvinale is a seasoned fine artist, performance poet, comedic storyteller, writer, cartoonist, photographer, and a small scale farmer living in beautiful Adams County. She has won numerous awards for her fine art, been in juried art shows and holds 7 awards for her poetry from the PA Poetry Society. In 2013 she took first place in a story telling contest featured in the Record Herald. She is currently published in The Messenger magazine, anthology book entitled Almost Time Enough; and had her own column in the Emmitsburg News Journal. She is a volunteer in a nonprofit nondenominational group of volunteers called Faith In Action, empowering and assisting people. In her spare time she entertains good people like you!

Ekta Rawat, a teenage author in Delhi has been published in a horror anthology, Horror Tales Transcending. Her work has been published in the national daily newspaper- The Pioneer, Amar Ujala , fortnight magazine Janpaksh and Political Science Journal of Lady Shri Ram College. She has served as a sub editor for the youth blog- fuccha, a writer for university media channel <u>dukhabar.com</u>. and senior interviewer at <u>venturesden.com</u>. Her guest submissions have featured in The Indian Economist, Writer Babu, Bring Home stories, Dainik Uttarakhand, The Car Dictionary and others. She believes that lenses of a new perception and bolts of creative compositions make up a travel cruise for all her readers.

Missi McLaren Ritter has used poetry in healing since she was a young girl. She has published 3 poetry collections, Chronicles of the Amazing Broken Girl, Bi-the-Way and Low Fat Love Poems. She has participated in several editing projects as a part of PoemSugar Press, Missi works with local art organizations to promote community and is a strong advocate for mental health awareness. She currently lives in York, PA, with her young son Nicholas and is working on her 4th poetry collection. For more information, you can visit Missi's website at <u>http://www.missiunedited.webs.com/</u>.

Theresa Rodriguez is a classical singer, poet, author and voice teacher. She previously taught music, voice and conducted the campus choir at Penn State Berks and is currently a member of the voice faculty of the Community School of Music and the Arts at the Goggleworks in Reading, Pa. She holds a Master of Music with distinction in voice pedagogy and performance from Westminster Choir College and is a member of the National Association of Teachers of Singing. Theresa is the author of Jesus and Eros: Sonnets, Poems and Songs. She is a contributing writer for Classical Singer Magazine where she writes on a variety of subjects of interest to classical singers. As a performance poet she has appeared as guest features as well as in the 2014 and 2015 Spoken Word Festivals of the Theater of the Seventh Sister of Lancaster. She has just published her fourth book Warning Signs of Abuse:

Get Out Early and Stay Free Forever which aims to help women get free early from abusive relationships. Theresa is the joyful mother of six children and grandmother to three grandsons. Her website is www.bardsinger.com.

Aylish Steed. I am a poet, a storyteller and an in-training Shamanic Practitioner. I am from Celtic roots of the Davidson and Innes Clans of Alba and of the Steed and Daines tribe, the Gypsy River Folk of the Fens. I have a deep connection with the land and the spirits of my ancestors. I have been writing since the age of eleven when poetry first began to inspire me. The ancient stories from our ancestors have been enchanting my soul since the tender age of five. My words come from the authentic nature of my heart and the vulnerable courage of my battle truth. I am the heroine of my life story; I am the fiery phoenix arising from the ashes, the beautiful butterfly breaking free from her cocoon. I am alive, I am dead, and I have been reborn.

Ogunsina Temi-tope (a.k.a Topid da Poet) is a performing poet from Oyo State, Nigeria whose performances and poetry address many societal issues and have been received both locally and internationally. Ogunsina started writing at age nine and has been featured in a number of anthologies: I Am Poetry (2013), Fearless Poets Against Bullying (2014), Emanation: Foray Into Forever (2014), and lnk Spot written collection (2014) and Poetry Society India anthology (2015)

Kera J. Valore Poetry for me has many facets. But, I am deep-rooted in the poems that express what I've endured throughout my life. I tend to bottle up emotions that haunt from the shadows. When I write a poem that taps into that vein, it's a huge weight lifted off me. It's first and foremost acknowledging, then reliving, and most importantly, releasing into the universe to carry. I used to feel embarrassed and ashamed to share these types of poems, but now I am empowered. I have removed myself from those who have hurt me and I am in a constant state of healing and repair. Poetry is just a part of that process.

T.L. Waid writes poetry and short fiction. She has been published in various anthologies. T.L. has published two collections and is currently working on her third. www.facebook.com/authorT.L.Waid

Kenneth Vincent Walker is a New Formalist Poet noted for his traditional and rhythmically lyrical style throughout South Central Pennsylvania. Considered a Performance Poet he can be seen throughout the region at various venues.

Lynn White lives in north Wales. Her work is influenced by issues of social justice and events, places and people she has known or imagined. She is especially interested in exploring the boundaries of dream, fantasy and reality. Her poem 'A Rose For Gaza' was shortlisted for the Theatre Cloud 'War Poetry for Today' competition in October 2014 and has since been published in the *'Poetry For Change Anthology* by Vending Machine Press.

Carol Clark Williams was third Poet Laureate of York, Pennsylvania. She teaches poetry workshops for high school students, senior citizen centers, support groups, and residents of prisons, halfway houses, and mental institutions. Her poems have been published in print and online journals including *Byline, Mad Poets Review, Manorborn, Margie, Fledgling Rag, The Pedestal,* and *Passenger.* She is the mother of two sons, a doctor at Temple Hospital and a rock musician.

Other books available from Community Arts Ink

Available at communityartsink.org and on Amazon

Reclaiming Our Voices